DON'T DO THIS
Learning from the Screw-Ups of Youth Ministry Leaders
by Len Kageler & Jonathan Hobbs

THE
YOUTH CARTEL

DON'T DO THIS

Publisher: Mark Oestreicher
Managing Editor: Tamara Rice
General Editors: Jonathan Hobbs and Len Kageler
Cover Design: Adam McLane
Layout: Marilee R. Pankratz
Creative Directors: Larry, Moe, and Curly

ISBN-13: 978-1-942145-24-0
SBN-10: 1-942145-24-1

The Youth Cartel, LLC
www.theyouthcartel.com
Email: info@theyouthcartel.com
Born in San Diego
Printed in the U.S.A.

From Jonathan...
To Pastor Bob Coats
and the First Baptist Church of Hightstown.
Thank you for hiring a young crazy kid as your youth director.
You allowed him to fail, but you never
let him see himself as a failure.

From Len...
To my wife Janet
who has often had to endure my being preoccupied
with cleaning up the ministry messes I have created.

CONTENTS

"When I was young, I observed that nine out of ten things I did were failures. So I did ten times more work."

George Bernard Shaw

INTRODUCTION

Both of us have experience the "highs" of ministry many times. The gospel has been shared. Hearts have stirred. Chains have been broken. Scars have been healed. Lives have been changed.

But both of us have made our share—or more than our share—of mistakes as well.

Jonathan nearly blew up a bunch of teens. (See Story 21.) And in an epic demonstration of magician prowess, he horrified a room full of teens when the straw that was supposed to disappear up his nose took a wrong turn. There was a lot of blood. (See Story 16.)

Len has several distinctive failures to his name. As far as we know, he is the only youth worker in all of Christendom to have ever scheduled a youth retreat in a house of prostitution. (See Story 38.) Another big one was losing $6,000 in one terrible night where not a single person came forward to hear more about the gospel at the evangelistic Christian rock star concert he'd confidently organized. Not one. (See Story 42.)

From Jonathan...
I was at my first church as youth director for three and a half years. I was actually hired there when I was only 19 years old. Not surprisingly, I failed. I failed a lot. I failed hard. I did events that almost no one came to. I spoke out of turn at church board meetings. I slept through my alarm and missed the Easter Sunrise Service where I was supposed to lead the music.[1] I tried to get teens to help me impress girls I wanted to date. I fell asleep during the church service. I fell asleep during a prayer meeting. (And I wasn't a quiet sleeper.) I insulted the church choir. Our youth group regularly left things damaged or broken. I didn't have tact. I had no appreciation for tradition. I didn't have any

---

1. I supposed this might technically be classified as a "win" in some circles.

understanding of the denomination. I had no respect for authority. I viewed the parents as my enemy.

From Len...

Being a rather confident and positive person, I always assumed that anyone who criticized my decisions was very simply ... wrong. Early in my ministry years the vibe I gave to any volunteers that happen to tolerate me was "You're here to hang out with teens and watch me do what I'm really good at."

I had some wake up calls along the way that eventually changed my heart. I was carrying all the sports equipment to our gym for the game night, and one of our volunteers looked at me in confusion and blurted out: "Len, don't you trust enough us to carry the sports gear to the gym?!"

My world stopped a few weeks later when a board member took me to lunch. He ran a billion dollar a year company. After some small talk he paused and said, "Len, you're pretty good working with the youth directly, but you have no idea how to work with others who work with them. We've talked about you as a board, and we think you are salvageable." (Gulp!!)

So this book is about failure, and we are grateful for all the youth workers who were willing to share their stories. But this book is about more than failure, it's a book of help and hope as well. Most of us learn something from failure. We all can gain wisdom through the experience of others.

Failure is a part of success. We've both heard it at youth leader conventions and leadership conferences. It's the topic of countless books, and it has even been the main point of Disney movies.[2] Creativity by its very nature produces more failures than successes. And youth ministry by its very nature is heavily dependent on creativity. But one of the things that can kill creativity is to focus only

---

2. *Meet the Robinsons*, dir. By Stephen J. Anderson (Walt Disney, 2007).

on the ideas that turned out to be good ones.

Perhaps you have heard the saying that "only one idea out of ten succeeds." And while that sentence is encouraging, it led us to think, "Shouldn't we then hear about failures more often?" At conventions we tend to hear all about successes. And if failures *are* mentioned, we only bring up the funny ones. But what about the others? What about the nine out of ten ideas that were awful?

This is a book about the other nine ideas. It is a collection of the stories that—though most were painful when they happened—have made each and every one of the authors better at what they do. Each story is told by the youth worker in his or her own voice. Some of the contributors offer lessons they've learned, and some let you glean the lessons yourself. Some are just a few sentences, and some are multiple pages long. The stories come from all over the country—and even a few from outside the US. We have divided them into five separate sections:

- Failures in the Fundamentals
- Failures with Youth
- Failures with Parents and Volunteers
- Failures with Church Leadership
- Failures that Defy Categorization

At the end of each section you will find questions for personal reflection or group discussion. We realize that a book like this may also be useful in a youth ministry class in a Christian college or university setting, or even in a seminary classroom. (After all, case studies are a big deal at Harvard!) We have supplied suggestions for major assignments that will deepen student learning. We suggest, if you are a youth ministry professor, that you have your students read these assignments early on, and then choose two or three of them as a substitute for a midterm exam or term paper.

This book is a place where failures are allowed. This is a book about the decisions we made that we'd like to take back. Sure, some of the stories are funny and will have you laughing out loud. Some of the stories will practically bring you to tears. Some of the stories may hit a little too close to home. But above all, our hope is that these stories communicate to you that you are not alone. We have been there. We all screwed up. And while we might be preaching to the choir, we *must* remember that we are more than the sum of our failures. We worship a holy God who seems to find a special joy in showing his glory through failures like you and me.

Len Kageler & Jonathan Hobbs
June 2016

"It is not a disgrace to fail. Failing is one of the greatest arts in the world."

Charles Kettering

"It's fine to celebrate success, but it is more important to heed the lessons of failure."

Bill Gates

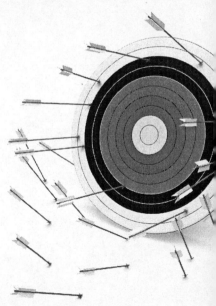

SECTION I
FAILURES IN THE FUNDAMENTALS

mistakes made in our own soul-care, our primary relationships,
or in understanding the ultimate purpose of youth ministry

SECTION I: INTRODUCTION

> "Failure isn't part of life, it's much of life. The rest is just learning how to grow from it."
>
> Bob Goff

Let's begin at the beginning, shall we? It's our guess that most of us choose to do youth ministry because we have some sense of calling. Perhaps that came about because God has placed a "burden on our hearts," something like the Old Testament Prophets. Amos, Isaiah, Jeremiah, you name 'em—it's like they had *no choice* but to prophesy. Or perhaps we've come to youth ministry, our calling to youth ministry, via spiritual gifts/strengths that work well with adolescents, and we've received positive affirmation from others along the way. It's not like we have this heavy "from on high" calling, but rather we feel God's pleasure, even his singing, over us when we are with youth.

Well, it's easy to see that just as with the Old Testament prophets and New Testament spiritual giftedness, ministry requires an ongoing connection with God. As we will see in this section, it is amazingly easy to let this piece of the picture get dim. After all, we're serving God, prepping for youth Bible studies or Sunday school lessons. We are (most likely) going to church regularly, singing the songs, smiling at people, and having the persona of a spiritual leader.

Why is it so important to keep our own soul fed? Well, aside from "practicing what we preach," there is the little issue of our reactions to youth misbehavior, parental criticism, or church board hesitancy to fund our latest Big Dream in ministry. If we are walking close to him, the fruit of the Spirit (Galatians 5:22-23) tends to be evident in our lives, even when things go bad.

From Len...
Unfortunately, I have been so dry spiritually that I swore at a teen when he stepped out of line. Another time I was too burned out to pay attention to what the teens were actually doing on an outdoor event. They were cliff-jumping 50 feet down into the lake. And yes, one was injured and required evacuation.

Foundations also refers to our primary relationships. If we've been so busy with youth ministry that our only actual friends are 15 and 16 year olds, we're headed for disaster. If we are married, and our spouse feels like they are a single because we are out so much "doing ministry," we will not long be married. It really is true that when we get married the spouse usually has the idea that we will still talk with them, be loving to them, and give evidence that they are important to us.

Many of us would agree that representing Jesus well in all his priorities is also foundational to Christian youth ministry. This includes having a heart to guide young people into a relationship with him and to help them be discipled into growing Christians who have a concern for their peers, their planet, and for Kingdom justice.

The authors of this section's stories reveal some gap, shall we say, in one or more of these foundational issues.

STORY 1: TEARS OF A HOCKEY PLAYER
by Andrew Root

The excitement and fear of being a brand new youth worker was consuming. I had just finished my first year on staff and would complete what I believed to be a successful start with a full bus headed to camp. I had been given 40 spots and told in no uncertain terms that filling these spots was important. But there were no reasons for worry; my bus was full and the anticipation was high as we drove four hours to camp. I felt I deserved extra credit points for not only filling my spots, but filling them with teens who had little to no connection with the church. I anticipated an exciting week watching a number of young people hear the gospel for the first time.

One of those teens was Adam. Adam was a 6'2", ninth grader who had played a leading role on his high school hockey team—which is no small accomplishment in Minnesota. He was as tough and mean as he was big. I felt particularly proud that I had convinced Adam to come to camp, figuring it reflected my own talent as a relational youth worker. I hoped that the claims of the gospel would make an impact on Adam's life.

But even I was surprised how quickly this seemed to happen. We had only been at camp a few hours, but here was Adam sitting alone, leaning against the wall, crying as the speaker talked about God's love. I did a double-take, not believing what I was seeing from across the room. Was Adam, the guy made of steel, really crying? It appeared that with every word of the speaker, Adam's head would lower, overwhelmed—I assumed with the love and mercy of God. Watching him from across the room, I thought what most youth workers would think; I even said to myself, "We got him!" I couldn't believe that hard-as-a-rock Adam had been melted by the heat of the gospel in just a few hours at camp.

As the program staff dismissed the teens, Adam sat, hands covering his face, trying to hide the tears. I waited for the room to clear, amazed at how easy youth ministry came to me, thinking that I was on my way to the youth worker hall of fame. When I felt the time was right I walked up to Adam, put my hand on his shoulder and asked if he wanted to take a walk. He looked at me with wet, red eyes and nodded.

We strolled around the property in silence for a while as I waited for Adam to gain some composure. Finally, I said to him, "So, what's up Adam?" I really didn't need to ask this question. I knew what was up; I knew perfectly well why he was crying. He had tasted the mercy and wonder of Jesus.

Adam cleared his throat, and wiping new tears that formed in his eyes, he said, "It's just…" stopping himself as the emotion would tighten his throat. Trying again he said, "It's just…" before again not being able to complete the sentence.

Impatiently, I completed the sentence in my mind: *It's just…JESUS. Come on Adam, just say it…* But the emotion seemed too heavy to allow these words to float to the surface. So as I waited, I imagined that after this night, when Adam confessed that all this emotion was glimpsing the beauty of the gospel, he would become a missionary, and in his biography, I would be worthy of mention. I figured it was a little arrogant to imagine that the chapter about me would be the first one or even in the first half of the book. But I assumed for sure I would have my own chapter.

Resting in the warmth of my own self-glorification, I asked one more time, "So what's up?"

This time Adam found the words and when they came, all my imaginary scenarios came crashing to the ground. Adam blurted out in deep pain, "She just doesn't even care that I exist!"

What? What? I thought to myself, *What is he saying? She doesn't even care that he exists? What?* I realized quickly that these tears had nothing to do with the speaker; he actually hadn't heard a word the speaker said. Like a scene in a movie, I was suddenly seeing flashbacks, Adam on the bus talking with Courtney, flirting with her, and then back to the day he signed up for camp. *Oh my gosh,* I thought to myself, as if the pieces of a mystery were coming together to reveal that I had known something all along but failed to see it. Courtney had signed up for camp first; it wasn't me at all. He was only here to make his big move. He'd loved Courtney since elementary school and had come to camp with visions of romance. Adam couldn't wait, and just minutes before the first meeting, where music and the gospel would be shared, he'd made his move, only to be shot down.

> ## DON'T DO THIS
>
> "I'd just finished up with my fifth and sixth grade class and was headed out the door for vacation when one of the girls asked to talk to me. I was walking (quickly) with her to my car, and I wasn't really paying attention. 'Bethany,' she lamented, 'I just don't know if I believe in God. I have these doubts and things just aren't making sense anymore.'
>
> 'No problem!' I exclaimed. 'You're young. You have plenty of time!' And I got in my car and drove away. I was 15 minutes down the road before my mind reviewed what had just happened. Had I seriously just said that?! (Yes... I've since followed up with her.)"
>
> Bethany Dixon

As I realized all this, I thought to myself, *You... you... stupid kid! Don't you realize that we're considering eternal things here and all you care about is this crush you won't care about in six months let alone six years!* Fortunately, I said nothing that night, but just walked with Adam, feeling badly that I had somehow done something wrong.

Reflecting now on that experience, I think I've learned something very important. While this experience of unrequited love felt banal to me, to Adam it was a deep experience, and one where questions, fears, and sufferings broke forth. I wanted to lead Adam into an experience with the living Christ, but what I missed that night, and have now come to see, is that this living Christ comes not in the transfer of information but directly in and through lived experience. That is, in moments of rejection, isolation, and death, the living Jesus comes to us, bringing his presence which promises to share in all of our humanity.

Early in my youth ministry days I wanted so badly for young people to *know* Jesus, but it wasn't until I learned to *be* with them, embracing their experiences, that I rediscovered that we, together, in and through this lived experience, encountered the living God who, in and through Jesus Christ, brings new life out of death.

I wish someone had told me back in those days to see my ministry as the invitation to join the lived experience of young people, entering their suffering and joy as a way of witnessing to the living God who comes to us often not in the words of the speaker but in the friendship that shares our suffering and embraces our humanity in the name of the humanity of God found in Jesus Christ.

STORY 2: FORGIVEN IDIOT
by Chap Clark

I was 19 years old and in college. I had been spending time at a local high school with the intent of building relationships and ultimately helping to starting a Christian club there. (This is back in the days where that was possible.) Since I loved Jesus, had been around good church youth groups, *and* I played pretty good guitar, basketball, and had huge hair, I felt like I could do this youth ministry thing.

The fall was great. I met a few guys who felt fairly comfortable around me. I met their parents, played basketball on weekends with them, and even taught a couple how to play guitar. In October we starting attending another school's club, so these four guys could see what one was like. By mid-November there was energy and excitement for us to start our own deal, and the four guys I'd first met with were at the center.

I invited them to go with me to an outreach weekend retreat. I felt a newfound missionary zeal, and as the camp approached, I was getting more and more excited about the possibility of these guys coming to faith. (None had ever been to church before and were pretty open, as were their parents.)

The weekend came. The first night's games were great, and the guys loved the talk—funny, inviting, and mildly introducing the person of Christ. We went back to our cabin and talked in a small group format (cleverly named "Cabin Time"), and the guys were enthusiastic to be there.

The next day, the wheels fell off.

In the morning after some more activities, the speaker to 500 high school youths, *at an outreach weekend retreat*, gave a talk describing "sin" and asked us to go back to our cabin and share with each other how we are "sinners." I think I understand what the speaker was trying to do, but he laid it on pretty thick and it didn't sit well with my guys. At the cabin, they just sat there and stared at me. They were all sophomores and had never heard anyone speak to them like that before. They were a dangerous mixture of angry and aghast.

I tried to engage them with innocuous statements like, "What's one thing you liked about the talk?"

Nothing. Silence.

"What was the speaker's main point?"

They looked at each other. Then it started.

"He said we were sinners, we were going to hell, and so were our parents." (For the record, I don't think he actually said either of those things, but that's how they heard it.)

"Is this why you brought us here, Chap? Is this why you've spent all this time with us, bought us food, played basketball with us?" I didn't hear these as questions as much as accusations. The tone of their voices showed that they were hurt, confused, and even felt betrayed.

Here's where I made my *mistake* (I've made many since, but this one does stick out): I got mad. Really mad. That they would turn on me like that, after "all I had done"! How dare they? Didn't they know that I had sacrificed hours and hours to start this club? Didn't they appreciate that I let them come to camp with me, and they had the opportunity to come to know *Jesus*?! *DIDN'T THEY GET THAT??!*

While many of us have these types of thoughts (even on somewhat of a regular basis), I did not allow them to simply be thoughts. They were words. I said them. Or more accurately, I yelled them.

The boys just sat there, stunned as I went on my rant. I tried to calm down, but they just looked at each other. Then they got up and left.

They wouldn't eat with me or participate in the large group mud game. They refused to go inside for the meeting that night.

At cabin time, I apologized. I asked for their forgiveness. They didn't really know what that meant, but they agreed. The rest of the weekend they were cold, quiet. Driving home nobody said a word. When we arrived at one of their houses, they all piled out, and one of them turned to me and said, "We forgive you. You mean well. You're just an idiot."

On Monday, that same guy called me and asked when their high school club was starting, and what the plan was. They were back. They were into it again. And they forgave me.

The club ended up a great success. It led to many teens coming to know Christ (including those four guys), and the ministry lasted for years after I moved on. But the best thing I learned throughout that season was the gift those guys gave me.

They told me the truth. I *had* manipulated them; I *had* used them. And they called me on it. They were right; I was an idiot. But I was a forgiven idiot, who was invited back into their lives.

STORY 3: "SORRY DEAR, SOMETHING MORE IMPORTANT CAME UP"

by Amy Jacober

I always thought there would be another chance. As a newly married woman, I was trying to find the balance of time for ministry and life. My husband booked a weekend at a bed and breakfast in Maine. Not only that, but he had to book it six months in advance. I had no idea how difficult the planning had been.

It all began with a lack of communication. I was a youth minister with a winter retreat planned and organized. I received a call from the venue saying they had a maintenance issue. We would have to reschedule. I knew there was no point fussing over the change. They had no control over the camp being shut down, and I know they never would have chosen to do so unless they had to. I put on my problem-solving hat and had a new venue, new date, and new plan in place within just a few days. The only thing I needed to do was get the word out to our families, and we were set. Oh, and check my own personal calendar. That would have helped tremendously.

It was only after sending out the new information to the church that my husband learned of the scheduling conflict. I panicked. I apologized to him and said I'd make it up to him. We'd have an amazing time whenever he was able to reschedule. I promised I wouldn't double book again.

In all fairness, he kept his cool and simply asked if one of two things could happen. Could I reschedule the youth retreat again explaining that I was busy? Or, could one of the other leaders take point on this one and I miss it?

I already felt guilty that I wasn't spending as much time with the youth as I had previously. Many of their families were integral in our dating, engagement, and marriage, and I wanted to pour back into them as much as they had supported us. I looked at our calendar and saw that there were no other free weekends until summer. I had great volunteers but none who felt like they could host a weekend with any spiritual depth. They offered to call it a time of fellowship and bonding, but I just couldn't let go of the lessons I had been taught over the years. You know the ones, where the moments of deep ministry are few and we need to take full advantage of every opportunity to create space for faith formation. To focus on hanging out and building friendships felt… well, less than holy at the time. In my mind, I had to be there.

We did have a retreat, and it was amazing! Truly, there were far too many sacred moments where God showed up for me to include in this writing.

What also took place was the hardest lesson on priorities that I have ever had. While we've had a great ride together, my marriage often revolves around ministry, and we've never made it to Maine. In fact, it's been a decade and we've never made it to a bed and breakfast anywhere. Ministry, three children, full-time work, and volunteering have filled our days. While we are blessed and happy, we can never get back that one trip that was so lovingly planned as a surprise for me. My husband has never tried a surprise again. I blew it, and I wish to this day that I could turn the clock back, trust the Holy Spirit more that the teens in my ministry would be just fine without me, and just take that weekend with the most important person in my life.

STORY 4: THE MONSTER INSIDE [3]
by Mark DeVries

Little did I know about the monster that decided to tag along on my first mission trip to Mexico.

I was just barely 20 years old, serving as an assistant youth director, deeply committed to being "radical for Christ," to pushing teens out of their comfort zone. I made it a point to meet with youth individually to challenge them in their discipleship, to pray with them, to push them to never settle for less than God's best in their lives.

Though we worked in 100-plus-degree heat every day, most mornings I led a group of our most committed youth on a pre-dawn jog for a few miles. Each night, we would go to a local park and do children's ministry there, as well as have our own time together as a group. Fifty teens or so traveling around Mexico on an old church bus (that I often drove) and keeping the youth motivated to work (many of whom seemed to require my perpetual prodding) made for ten very intense days. But I loved every minute of it. Well, almost every minute.

In our evenings at the park, the guys in the group would throw together a quick, full-contact football game (as if we needed more exercise!). And each night, I would line up against the same guy. He was much bigger than me, much more muscular, and seemed to relish the opportunity to throw me to the ground, which he did with infuriating consistency.

On one of the last nights of the trip, we returned again to our football ritual. Before long, things had moved from frustrating to tense, as the guy across the line continued to pummel me after every snap. As I returned to the line for what would be the last time, my grid-iron adversary observed my anger rising and responded with a smirk, "You know I'm going to hit you again, don't you?" When the ball was snapped, so did I.

I jumped across the line with my arms flailing, fists searching for any target I could find on my tormentor. As the slack-jawed teens watched my demonstration of Christian love in action, I yelled a few angry words at my opponent and stormed off.

At least it wasn't a teen I was attacking or a parent.

It was just my boss.

The youth director pulled me aside, taking me on a long walk as slowly, very slowly, I calmed down. I would like to say that a light bulb went off in my head and I immediately realized that I was not living at an emotionally healthy pace on that trip. But it was too easy to focus on my boss's taunting, rather than to deal with a pattern that was to become increasingly clear over the next decade: my own lack of self-care and boundaries, a drive that I excused in the name of being wildly committed to following Christ.

STORY 5: FUNDRAISER GONE WRONG
by Alisa Laska

I learned a lot of things from my first full-time position. The most important lesson was to always look at ministry as a mission field. Each church that you work for will likely be in a different area with different people and a very different culture. What worked in one context won't always work in another. One youth group may love a certain game and another will hate it. In one area the youth are focused on sports and college preparations; in another they'll be out duck-hunting and mud-bogging. Inevitably, that "great idea" you had in one church could be the worst idea ever in your next job.

For my first part-time position, I had worked in the Philadelphia suburbs, full of upscale cafés, musicians, country clubs, and art museums. Four years later, I moved to the South, where the culture was more relaxed, friendly, and seemed to revolve around food. And the food was either fried or (my church's favorite) barbeque. Being from the North, I understood barbeque to be cooking hot dogs and hamburgers on the grill. Down South, barbeque meant something entirely different. There was also perlow, fried chicken, collard greens and biscuits. (When the church announced their perlow[4] dinner, I did not attend, because I didn't know what it actually was!) There is

---

4. It's a Southern rice dish that includes bacon, onion, celery, green pepper, tomatoes, Cajun seasoning, and... well... other wonderful things. Look it up online. It's fantastic.

so much glorious food that they even have a term for the weight a Northerner gains when they move down there: The "Yankee Fifteen."

After I worked for the church for a few months, we began talking about fundraisers to support our annual summer mission trip. When I asked around, one of our volunteers, who really knew a lot about the church culture, told me that we should have a pig roast. I almost laughed in her face (bless her heart). I honestly thought she was joking. *You wanted me to roast an actual pig?* I pictured a large animal stretched out over an open flame and started to cringe. She explained how last year a member of our church brought his "pit" (another new term for me) up to the parking lot and we made over $500.

Wow... $500? That was a good profit. But I didn't know the first thing about barbeque. If I was going to plan this thing, I thought I should at least have some basic knowledge of it. I thanked her for the idea, but went back to my office and quickly forgot it.

As the image of a roasting pig faded from my mind, I went online and started looking for musicians. I decided that what we needed was a good country musician to come and play at the church. We could advertise all around town, and lots of folks would come. I knew we could raise more than $500 for our mission trip. After all, everyone loves music, right? And all Southerners like country, right? In my last church, we'd had coffeehouses where the youth would perform and some professional musicians would come and play and we'd make over $1,000 per night.

I asked some of my Philly musician friends for a suggestion, and they

DON'T DO THIS

"One of our teens and I were both looking forward to March Madness. We saw each other at church on 'Selection Sunday' which is when the brackets come out for the tournament. I gave her a high five and said, 'I'm so exited!'

'Me too!' she said. 'This is the second best Sunday of the year!'

I looked at her confused. 'What's the best Sunday? Super Bowl?'

She looked at me disgusted. 'Easter, Jesse... Easter.'

Oh... right... Easter. Because we love Jesus... I knew that. Oops."

Jesse Parker

recommended a guy who played bluegrass and folk music on guitar.
I checked out some of his music online, and I really liked him. He
was good at what he played and I knew the folks in the church would
love him too. I told the volunteer (the pig roaster) about it. I was very
excited as I told her my plans to bring in the musician and make lots
of money.

She looked at me a bit skeptically. She mentioned again that the
nice man in the church could just pull up his smoker and we'd make
$500 easily for the youth. These folks like to eat, she reminded me.
I said yeah, I'd keep that in mind, but went on with my plans for the
concert.

I pulled out the church credit card and booked the musician. As the
planning progressed, I booked his transportation and lodging in
town, made flyers and had them printed at the local printer. I took
a youth with me and put up signs in the local shop windows. I put
blurbs in the church bulletin and stood up and made announcements
in front of the congregation.

The big night finally arrived. I had lots of youth coming to help out by
selling tickets and refreshments. Leaders were on hand to help where
needed. The musician arrived and we all enjoyed talking to him. He
was a natural storyteller.

As the start time drew closer, a few people rolled in. By a few, I mean
literally five people. Five. I started to panic a little. Just a little. I
thought to myself, this is the South, maybe they are just taking their
time getting here. Maybe they thought it was 7:30 instead of 7:00.
I delayed the start time by 15 minutes, thinking it would help, but
only one more person showed up. Finally, I gave the go ahead to the
musician, and he began to play.

From the first strums of his guitar, we were captivated by his playing
and the stories he told through his words. He was great. I only wished
there were more than six people there to hear him.

During intermission, I went up and to give him his payment check.

He said he felt bad even taking it, because he knew this was supposed to be a fundraiser. I appreciated his concern, but told him not to worry about it. I felt like that was my problem… not his. It was a great night of music, but a disappointing fundraiser.

I suppose that's what happens when we stop listening to the wisdom of others, and stop being students of the culture in which we serve. Missionaries get to know their people… their food, their interests, what they do in their free time. They check out the ministry context and minister with culture in mind. If they are good, they don't bring their own culture with them and impose it on people. They let the culture form their ministry. This is where I went very wrong. I used the word "I" too much. *I* have this great musician I'd like to bring in. *I* think we'll make lots of money. *I* want to try this. I had been what I'd consider "successful" during my four years of ministry in Philadelphia. But when I arrived down South, I had a whole lot to learn about the culture. Sadly, I didn't do enough listening.

STORY 6: "SHE DOESN'T UNDERSTAND"
by Ron Belsterling

I've often found ways to laugh at my mistakes. Not this time. Sacrificing one's family for the ministry was on my radar. I was well aware of the horror stories. I was *sure* I would *not* let that happen in my home. In the several interviews I had with different churches over the years, I made it *clear*: "I will not sacrifice my family for the ministry." And then, my wife said those words that I'll never forget; they hit me deeper than I've ever been hit by anyone.

"Ron, do you remember years ago, before we were married, you told me that you wanted us to have a love that was committed and not love based on emotion that comes and goes? We agreed that we would tell each other when the feelings weren't there." And then she said, "I will always be committed to loving you. And you need to know that right now, I have no feelings of love for you. You have time for everyone but me. You've told me (gratefully) that I'm the only one who understands. Well, I don't. I need a husband who spends time with me. But know I will always be committed to you."

I would like to say my immediate response was mature. It wasn't. I felt sorry for *myself*, not her. I was killing myself. I had built the ministry to the largest in the district. I was working on a PhD in *family* studies, and teaching university classes. I was a *marriage* and *family* therapist. I had three little ones who demanded my attention the minute I walked in the door. I was working extra jobs to pay bills. I always counted on my wife understanding. Understanding what? Essentially, that I had no time for her.

No wonder she didn't feel love for me. For more than a year, she was hardly a part of my life. I am so grateful to my wife for having the courage to say those words, which had to be tremendously difficult for her to say. By God's whispers as well, I heard my wife's pain. I had to do something. And it had to be drastic.

I quit the counseling job (at that point, I wasn't well-suited for it anyway). I refused to answer the phone after I got home from work. I started delegating not only secondary responsibilities, but primary ones. I did not need to be involved in every youth ministry activity. If people asked me (the youth minister) to do things not on the schedule, then I started saying no or "not this year."

I realized *no one* (aside from the Holy Spirit) would help me make my wife a priority.

The church body and the youth weren't going to help me. "Pastor Ron, I only need ten minutes." Everyone in the church wants us to make our families a priority, until their personal phone call is not answered. People simply have no idea of the demand for attention the church body has or that teens have.

The senior pastor wasn't going to help me. In my time in youth ministry, the senior pastors I worked for frequently had me do so many things not even close to my job description, and would often dump requests/service/etc. on me at the last minute. No longer.

Very soon after my wife shared her pain with me, my senior pastor wanted me to do an activity with my youth, which we had just done. It simply was too awkward to fit it again into the vision and flow of the ministry. And it was on a day that I had committed to my wife, that I reserved for her. When he found out that my biggest hesitancy was because of family plans, he demanded I adjust them. I told him that I wouldn't. He demanded again. I told him to do what he had to, but I would not change my schedule. (He ended up leading the trip and was robbed while on it. Needless to say, he was even less happy about it all.)

My children weren't going to help me. They were simply too young to understand. I was the biggest, bestest toy in the house. And, they already had to share me with all the teens and families and my other responsibilities.

My wife wasn't going to help me. When she found out about the senior pastor wanting me to change our family plans and that I told him I wouldn't, she begged me to adjust them. She begged me to do the event. Literally. I was floored. And I told her, "Honey, I'm making you a priority. You just told me you needed me to do this." She said, yes, but not now. Due to her fears related to the immaturity of the senior pastor, she had caved. She was being sacrificial on my behalf— willing to give up in the short term, what she didn't want for the long term.

The problem is the short-term "opportunities" often demand payment from the long-term vision. I changed my approach to ministry about as abruptly as one can. I am so grateful to my wife that she spoke words I didn't want to hear. I am so grateful to God that he shed his light into my life and helped me to trust him with the changes. My wife and children are grateful too.

STORY 7: THE YES MAN
by Ryan Sidhom

It was my first day on the job in my first ministry position, and I knew that I had one simple goal. I don't know if I would have put it in these terms, but in retrospect it's definitely the truth. *I wanted to be a hero.*

I wanted people to love me and the work I was doing. Our youth group would quadruple in size. My picture would be in the paper. People would come from miles around to learn my "secret." I'd be asked to publish articles. I'd write books. I'd speak in front of thousands of people about how to do youth ministry better. *All shall love me!!!*[5]

I even had a very basic plan to reach this goal, and it wasn't in any way, shape, or form biblical or spiritual. And just like with my desire to be the hero, I'm not sure I would have phrased it this way back then, but nevertheless it was what I set out to do. Simply put, I would make everyone happy.

The senior pastor made it clear he wanted me to stay busy doing a lot of stuff with the youth. The teens themselves all suggested that the former youth director didn't have enough fun things on the calendar.

---

5. Yes, I was going for a *The Lord of the Rings* reference there… hope you enjoyed it.

The parents seconded that notion and even added to it, wanting both "youth only" activities *and* events for the whole family. To top it all off, I had more than one senior citizen member of our church stop by my office to tell me stories of how the last youth pastor didn't keep the youth busy enough, and so their idle teenage hands became the devil's tools (passing notes in church, not cleaning up after themselves... awful, sinful things like that). But they assured me that they knew that I was going to be different.

I wanted to be different. I wanted to be a hero. To that end I wanted to make everyone happy. But how could I make people happy?

Stuff. Doing lots and lots of *stuff*. I decided to say yes to any and every opportunity that ever came across my path. Our calendar would be full. Our hands would not be idle. Genius.

To any veteran youth pastor reading this, you already know how this story ends. This is a terrible idea. Beyond terrible in fact. But if I were reading this 15 years ago, I probably would have thought, "This is absolutely brilliant!"

So I bypassed all of the learning curves (because none of them applied to me), and after only two weeks at my first youth ministry position, I became the best and the brightest youth pastor to ever walk the planet. I became the yes man.

A teen approached me and mentioned that he wanted to do a study on the end times, so I started a series on Revelation. Another wanted advice on sex and dating and "how far is too far?" That led to me starting another series on relationships. Never mind the fact that both of these topics were not my specialty and required a ton of study and planning on my part. The youth also decided that I needed to change up the look of the meeting space more often, so I obliged.

A parent approached me and suggested that we do a lock-in. Done. It was a "success" (nobody died and 911 only got prank called once). This unfortunately led to more and more suggestions. Youth started begging to do extra events every week. Due to all of this activity, I was asked to do fundraisers. (None of which raised any funds. Or fun.)

The requests started coming in at an unbelievable pace. On top of all of that, people were asking to make the ministry *larger*. The college youth wanted to be a part of the youth ministry, and they had event ideas of their own. The sixth graders wanted to be folded into the youth ministry as well. This also came with more ideas and suggestions.

Before I knew it, I was running around like a mad man doing a whole lot of stuff that never made a difference in anyone's life, let alone the Kingdom. I was constantly behind on everything that *really* mattered (if I ever even got around to it). I had allowed myself to be consumed with all of the "stuff" of ministry that really *didn't* matter.

I allowed myself to be consumed with a lie. I had bought into the idea that *busy* equals *better*. Filling our schedules only ended up making everybody frustrated and angry. I learned the hard way that it's a lot more difficult to say no to something after you've already said yes to it. In hindsight, I wish I had given all of the suggestions and requests more time and prayer before hastily agreeing. Even if I didn't say no, a "let me pray about it" would have been better.

One of the biggest dangers of the "yes-to-everything" mindset is that it oftentimes left prayer out of the equation. Instead of praying about the direction of the ministry, I allowed the voices of others to dictate what I did. Obviously, there's nothing wrong with seeking godly counsel before making a decision (in fact, we are commanded to do so), but I can't pretend that this was what I was doing.

Most importantly, I thought I was *way more important* than I actually was. Now, I work hard to make sure that Jesus is the only hero there is in my ministry. I tried being the guy that everybody liked. I tried to be the guy that could solve all of the problems. Consequently, I ended up being the guy that hardly anybody liked. I was the guy that caused more problems than there were to begin with.

I wish I had said no more. Or even better, I wish I had simply said,

DON'T DO THIS

"Let me pray about it and seek some godly counsel."

Prayer is a "no duh" thing, right? Imagine how much better off we'd be if we actually did it.

STORY 8: PERSONAL RESPONSIBILITY
by Brock Morgan

I entered college as a PE major. Mostly, I think, because I wanted to play dodgeball for the rest of my life. But over my freshmen year of college God really got a hold of my life, ultimately ruining all of my plans. That was 24 years ago, and I've been doing youth ministry ever since. As I look back on those years, I'm blown away how God has even used a person like me.

The past few summers we have had former students visit us who were a part of our ministry over those twenty-some years, and each time, inevitably, the stories start coming. The stories of God working are my favorite, but my former youth seem to like telling and retelling the times that I made a fool of myself or the times I got in trouble. I just sit there cringing and think, "Man, was I stupid!" So here are a few cringe-worthy moments for your pleasure… and hopefully for you to learn what not to do:

I was 23 years old and in my first full time ministry position. My intern, and fellow driver, was my best friend from elementary school. We were heading out of Los Angeles in our church vans full of middle school youth. We began racing through traffic, trying to beat each other to the condos we had rented for the weekend. Not only was this dangerous, but we had a mom following us with my wife sitting in the van with her. I remember "mom" making us pull off to the side of the road and yelling at us in front of all of the teens. Thanks to "mom" (you know who you are) for that much needed lecture, but talk about humiliating.

Then there was the time I had one of our volunteers hide in the false ceiling of the youth room with a fire extinguisher full of water. With a loud crash he dropped out of the sky, made a perfect landing on the stage, and hosed everyone down. We found out later that one of the teens had to be rushed to the doctor for fear of a detached retina. He had been squirted in the eyeball at point-blank range.

Or how about my first parents' meeting? I spoke to a room full of amazing parents who sat there listening to me go on and on as if I knew, at 23, how to parent teenagers. I remember this gracious mom coming up to me afterwards and saying, "Brock, you don't have a clue what you're talking about!" The funny thing is, I didn't. I had never raised a child, and I had never lived full time with a 13 year old. As the parent of a teen now, I am a much better youth worker.

I remember one year going to the Youth Specialties National Convention and hearing Tony Campolo use the "S" word. I thought he was so cool, so I decided to pull that one out for our youth group back home. Let me just say this: Teenagers tell their parents everything we youth workers do, especially if it will shock their parents. Campolo was much more effective than I was. The next day my pastor called me in for a meeting that would be a huge wake-up call.

But the one that takes the cake was when I was asked to come and speak at a local Christian high school. The topic they wanted me to speak on was "personal responsibility." Maybe you already got this, but "personal responsibility" hasn't always been my strong suit. So, my wife and I headed out to this school that I had never been to with directions written on a napkin by a 15-year-old youth. Needless to say, we got lost. With about ten minutes left until I was supposed to speak and knowing that we were a good 20 minutes away, I started to speed. I remember my wife saying, "Brock, if you get a ticket, I am going to kill you." My response was, "Baby, we're fine. There's no way I'll get a ticket." Then, to my surprise, flashing lights were in the rear view mirror and a siren was blasting behind the car. We pulled over and the police officer walked up to my wife's side of the car, so she rolled down her window. He pointed at me and said, "Get out of the car buddy, you're going to jail! We've been chasing you for ten minutes on both sides of the freeway, and you're in big trouble." My wife started crying, and not just little tears. She was balling her eyes out, and furious to boot.

I got out of the car and the officer reached for his handcuffs. In a shaky voice I said, "Sir, please don't arrest me. I'm a youth pastor and I'm supposed to speak at a Christian school down the road on 'personal responsibility.' Please don't take me to jail. *Please!*" God was with me that day, my friends. The officer paused for a second, put his cuffs away, and said, "Get back in your car." My wife took one look at me and, with evil in her eyes, slugged me right in the gut. The officer wrote me a ticket and gave me directions to the school. I walked in, still shaking, as the worship band finished their last song. I got on the stage and talked about the importance of being responsible, with a great analogy, I might add. How ironic.

I am one of those youth workers who have had to learn the hard way. These are funny stories, and they are moments that I look back on in wonder. But I don't tell you this to make light of some awful moments in my ministry life. I truly wasn't ready to be a minister when I began. But I can tell you this, I love young people and I love seeing Jesus change their lives. I've just found I need to get out of the way a bit and let him have his way with them. And if God can use me, he can use anyone.

STORY 9: THE COST OF CONFLICT AVOIDANCE
Name Withheld

I have no doubt that many of the stories submitted for this book will be funny, so I suppose it's appropriate that I give you, the reader, a quick heads-up. My story won't make you laugh. You will probably find it disturbing. My hope is that sharing this story helps lead us to a future where these things just don't happen anymore.

It's probably best to come right out and state the shocking punch of the story: The head of our youth ministry, whom I'll refer to here as "Tom," was accused (and found guilty) of molesting youth and leaders. He initially confessed to only one incident, but subsequently pled guilty to nearly a dozen charges of varying severity. He was married with children.

Was this story a failure on my part? No. I had been unaware of his behavior until he was caught. But… yes. Perhaps it was a failure of sorts on my part. I was not the senior pastor, but I was Tom's boss and the one who hired him. There are things I might have done that could have helped him and, by extension, his eventual victims.

I was stunned. Tom had a thriving ministry. He was well reg? the community. He was a gifted speaker and a strong leade him to be relentless—and sometimes borderline legalistic regard to the personal holiness of his volunteer staff. He threatened to dismiss a volunteer leader for getting her eyebrow pierced. The idea of him having had an inappropriate relationship floored me.

But that morning the horrific truth tumbled out. He was having a sexual relationship with one of his young volunteer leaders—the son of a board member, no less. After months, perhaps years, of being subjected to Tom's physical and emotional manipulation, the young leader had finally told his father about it. Tom had been caught, and he had called me only an hour before I would have been informed by the young man's father. I accepted Tom's resignation on the spot.

I met with Tom several times in the weeks that followed. I spoke with our Human Resources staff and committee daily. I consulted with our ministry's attorney weekly. And I begged Tom to tell me the full story. Had there been others with whom he'd had a relationship? The young leader was over 18 years old so this was technically not felonious behavior. But what if there had been younger boys? To protect any possible victims, our ministry, and Tom's family, I needed to know.

Tom confessed to a few things that had nothing to do with our ministry and which had no legal ramifications. These were relationships with adult men in other cities. I interpreted his confession of these things as evidence that he was being honest with me. After all, I would never have found out about these other incidents if he had not told me. I told our HR department that I believed that we had reached the bottom of it all.

A month later, another member of my staff accompanied a young man into my office. This college freshman had been in Tom's high school ministry for four years and he had suffered both physical and devastating emotional abuse from him. I instantly called the police and a thorough investigation began. Four months later Tom was arrested on eleven counts involving seven young men. The news was on every TV network in our city, and it was on the front page of every newspaper. A year later, Tom pled guilty to the charges in exchange for a more lenient sentence.

There was a lot of damage, but by God's grace there was also a lot of healing for the victims. The ministry survived. And shockingly, so did Tom's family.

In the years that followed, I was asked several times by well-meaning people, "Do you feel at all responsible for what happened? Do you feel like you should have known?" My answer has always been no. Even his wife didn't know, so how could I have known?

But there is one thing I have lost sleep over: I knew *other* things. They were not horrific, and they were by no means grounds for termination, nor perhaps even grounds for alarm. But they were significant, nonetheless.

I knew that Tom was manipulative. I had seen it all too many times. He always seemed to get what he wanted no matter the cost to others. I knew that Tom never lost an argument. He'd cleverly change the subject rather than back down. I knew that Tom was not always honest. He had recently been caught in a small lie that had alienated a few volunteer leaders. I also knew that Tom had an arrogant streak.

Because the things that I saw were small concerns and isolated incidents, and because he was effective in ministry and surrounded by a large cadre of adults and leaders in his community who believed in him, I figured that the people "on the ground" knew better than me. And frankly, I did not want to have a confrontation with a man who was manipulative and arrogant. I knew that such a confrontation was bound to be unpleasant. As many times as I thought about doing it, I always found reasons to avoid it.

Conflict and *confrontation*—these are words that I've always hated. Perhaps my abhorrence has been a product of my difficult upbringing. To survive adversity at home, I became a "people pleaser." But as an adult, my life and my ministry came to be defined by an avoidance of conflict at nearly any cost. In fact, as I look back on my first 20 years of ministry, nearly every difficulty that I experienced was somehow related to my reluctance to speak difficult truths to people.

When I was moving into my current position many years ago, my mentor met with me and gave me some fantastic advice that I wish I had taken to heart back then. I hope it echoes as true for you as it has for me: *Confront people problems when you see them. Don't wait. Because people problems never go away; they only get bigger and uglier. It's not a question of whether or not you will deal with them. It's only a question of when you will deal with them, and how bad they will get between now and when you do.*

SECTION I: REFLECTIONS

Paden Gullquist @KeepThingsPG   April 8
I may or may not have accidentally locked a kid in
church and left earlier. #oops #youthministryfail

One thing that struck us about these stories is how the mistake, be
it in what you might call soul care, primary relationships, or basic
ministry understandings impacted not only the author but those
around them. We find it interesting what stories different people find
the most powerful. We are both married (Len to Janet and Jonathan
to Carolyn) and the stories that had to do with failure in that regard
were particularly compelling. The stories brought up some unhappy
personal memories.

From Len...
I had a similar experience as Ron when my wife informed me that
she no longer loved me, since I had seemingly chosen my job over
her. Over the years several other youth pastors have told me of similar
stories. (By the way, my wife and I have been married several decades
now. She forgave me, and I have worked hard to help our marriage
flourish.) Another low for me was one Christmas morning when
my young children were screaming at me "Wake up, Daddy!" I was
so exhausted from ministry events that I fell asleep while opening
presents!

From Jonathan...
I have witnessed the marriages of multiple youth ministry colleagues
fall apart at the expense of such mistakes. These were couples that
everyone saw as "perfect for each other" and "partners in ministry." But
the slow erosion power of putting our ministries over our loved ones
can wear down solid foundations and deteriorate the deepest of roots.

You'll be interested to know Len has done some tracking about full-time youth workers who get fired and for what reasons. Back in 1992, he surveyed 185 youth pastors who had been fired from their positions, and 29% of them lost their jobs due to immorality—defined as inappropriate relationships with other staff/adults or unethical conduct with (or even in more rare cases sexual abuse of) youth.[6] Youth Specialties asked Len to do the research again in 2008, to see if there had been any changes in the stats. Interestingly, while the number one reason youth pastors get fired remained unchanged (some kind of conflict, 49% in both 1992 and 2008) the percentage of those who lost their jobs due to immorality (however broadly defined) went from 29% down to 6%.[7] Those of us who teach youth ministry in colleges and seminaries would like to think that part of this rather spectacular decline is due to the fact that moral failure is something we all talk about and teach about now.

We seek to help future youth workers realize *they* are at risk, and we must have radical accountability when it comes to our moral integrity—whether it's our thought lives, our online viewing habits, our interactions with young people themselves, and our marriages.

Some of the problems in the foundations area stem from our own personal immaturity. We're certain that many reading these pages have a basic understanding of adolescent development. Neuroscience tells us that the pre-frontal cortex is the part of the brain where risk assessment, analytical skills, planning, foreseeing consequences, and application of "lessons learned" comes from. Neuroscience also tells us that some of us don't have a fully functioning pre-frontal cortex until our mid to late 20s. It's clear many of the youth workers who wrote here are not only mature enough now to see their youthful actions as mistakes, but they've come to a place in life where they are unlikely to make those mistakes again.

---

6. Kageler, Len. *The Youth Minister's Survival Guide: How to Recognize and Overcome the Challenges You Will Face* (Grand Rapids: Zondervan/Youth Specialties, 1992).
7. Kageler, Len. *The Youth Ministry Survival Guide: How to Thrive and Last for the Long Haul* (Grand Rapids: Zondervan/Youth Specialties, 2008). This book is a revised and updated version of *The Youth Minister's Survival Guide* (see note 6).

This personal immaturity is not an excuse, of course, for *breaking bad* in one or more of these foundational areas. If we are young ourselves, the need to intentionally listen to and intentionally apply the lessons others have learned becomes more urgent. When we were younger, we both had the attitude that bad things happened to other people, but certainly we were exempt. Not so, it turns out. No one is exempt.

Questions for Reflection or Discussion

1. All modesty aside, which of the three areas (soul care, primary relationships, or basic ministry understanding), seems to come the easiest for you and why?

2. Sometimes people in ministry think "Since I am busy doing God's work, my soul will take care of itself," but it's a notion Mark Oestreicher labels a *seductive misconception*. How have you bought into this misconception yourself? How have you seen this misconception in others?

3. Have you, or someone you know, ever misinterpreted adolescent emotion/needs the way Chap and Andrew did in Stories 1 and 2? What did that look like?

4. Take another look at the fruit of the Spirit in Galatians 5:22-23. What adolescent behavior triggers a "non-fruit" reaction in you? How do you intend to stay continually close to the Spirit as you engage in spiritual youth ministry? In other words, how do you or will you care for your own soul?

Major Project Ideas for the Classroom

1. Compare and contrast the personal impact of five free online devotionals. (Searching for "daily devotionals" will yield ample hits.) Try several for several days each and compare them using criteria such as: a) its effectiveness in connecting you to the Word, b) its practical application to your personal life, and c) its potential application to those in ministry.

"Failure should be our teacher, not our undertaker. Failure is delay, not defeat. It is a temporary detour, not a dead end. Failure is something we can avoid only by saying nothing, doing nothing, and being nothing."

Denis Waitley

"It is impossible to live without failing at something, unless you live so cautiously that you might as well not have lived at all, in which case you have failed by default."

J. K. Rowling

2. Complete Idea 1 using devotional books instead of online tools.

3. Obtain and read the books *What's Your God Language?* by Myra Perrine[8] and *Made to Pray* by Chris Heinz.[9] Write a two-page personal application paper for each book and prepare a 60- to 90-minute soul care seminar/experience for volunteer youth workers.

---

8. Perrine, Myra. *What's Your God Language?: Connecting to God Through Your Unique Spiritual Temperament* (Carol Stream, IL: Tyndale, 2007).
9. Heinz, Chris. *Made to Pray: How to Find Your Best Prayer Types* (Bloomington, IN: WestBow Press, 2013).

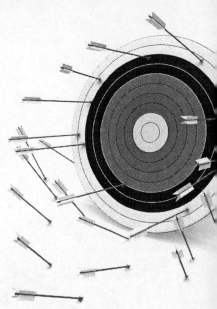

SECTION II
FAILURES WITH YOUTH

mistakes made in programming events, responding
to the unexpected, relating to youth, and understanding
adolescent perspective

SECTION II: INTRODUCTION

> "The greatest glory in living lies not in never falling, but in rising every time we fall."
>
> Ralph Waldo Emerson

One thing that brought both of us to youth ministry is that we both enjoyed youth... being with them, laughing with them, traveling with them, having new experiences with them, seeing them grow up (literally) before our eyes, and seeing them come to and grow in Christ. In most of the stories in this section, the joy of being with youth is front and center!

Another, related thing that brought both of us to youth ministry is that many of the things we plan with or for teens are things that *we ourselves enjoy doing*. How cool is it to get paid to ski at Whistler Mountain, BC (site of the 2010 Olympics), go jet-skiing, attend major Christian music festivals, travel internationally, and use church buildings in ways that the saints who paid for (and in many cases built) them could not have imagined nor would probably approve?

But, alas, amid all this fun, sometimes things don't go as planned. This section, unlike the previous one, has a great deal of humor, though some stories are very serious.

STORY 10: STICKING WITH THE LESSON PLAN, DESPITE ARMAGEDDON
by Mark Oestreicher

Several years ago, I was working as the youth worker in a church just northeast of Los Angeles. It was the year people in Los Angeles said our four seasons were earthquakes, riots, floods, and fires. We had 'em all. And the fires (brush fires in the mountains) were very, very close to my church. Schools were closed, houses were burning, ash was falling from the sky like snow. It was all very Armageddon-like.

Our young teen group met on the evening of the worst day. Something was happening in our normal meeting space, so we met in a room on the top floor of the church that had huge windows facing the directions of the fires. One of the girls who attended that night had lost her home and everything in it to fire that day. She was in shock and didn't have anywhere else to go, so her parents brought her to church. Several others present had been evacuated from their homes and were waiting to hear if their homes had burned down or not.

As we met, we could see palm trees burst into flames (they go up like fireworks!) and the occasional home burning.

And Mark Oestreicher, idiot youth worker, stuck to his lesson plan.

I could have had the group discuss their emotions about this and then have an extended time of prayer, or I could have led a Bible study regarding "turning to God when disaster hits." We could have even all gone to the local convenience store to purchase snacks and juice for firefighters. Just about anything other than going on as planned would have been an improvement.

I know. I said I was an idiot. Stop repeating it.

I offer this rather extreme example to reveal an often more subtle misconception many youth workers live with: my teaching plans, my program, my plans of any kind, once prepared and ready to go, will remain the best course.

Here's a truth I've come to embrace: My best spiritual discussions with teenagers are *very rarely* connected to whatever I have planned. My best spiritual discussions—really my best ministry times of any sort—occur naturally in the thin-places of life. When I hold my plans loosely, waiting on God's spirit and the realities of my teenagers' lives… well… that's when the good stuff shows up.

STORY 11: REMEMBERING I'M NOT A PSYCHOLOGIST
by Jonathan Hobbs

Years ago I had a girl in youth group that was a "cutter" (she would self-harm or cut herself, normally on her wrists, not to kill herself but finding a type of emotional relief in self-harm). This is somewhat of a common problem in the world of adolescent psychology these days, but back then, it was lesser known. I had little-to-no training on dealing with it, but I decided to level with her. I told her that I had heard about her struggle (she never told me directly) and that I wanted to help in any way I could—but I didn't know how... so I needed her to let me know what I could do.

She denied that there was an issue anymore and was obviously embarrassed and rattled at my direct approach. She said she had to go to the bathroom and left my office.

I was in the middle of another discussion when she came back about five minutes later. She yelled "How about *this?* Is *this* helping, Jon?!" At this point she held up her arm, which was covered in blood, and then she ran down the stairs and out the door.

There was a billboard next to the bathroom. She had grabbed a thumb tack off of the board and dug it into her arm multiple times.

I will never forget that image.

I tried to chase after her, but she was already gone. I called her mom and explained what had happened.

I jumped into water that was way too deep for me on that day. It was all well intended, but it was a terrible approach. It didn't occur to me to talk with the mom first (and try and partner with her). It didn't occur to me to talk to a professional and get advice from them. I just jumped in… and nothing good came of it.

STORY 12: "STOP THE MOVIE!"
by Tic Long

My story takes place way back in the late '70s, but I'm pretty sure that some version of this still happens all over the place. Apparently we just never learn.

I was running a junior high ministry in Oakland, California, and we decided to do a big outreach event on the night of Halloween. We figured it would be awesome to do an all-night Halloween party. Yes, I know. We were crazy.

We averaged about 40 teens a week at youth group, but this event brought in over 90. We had never met over half of the youth attending. As bad as that was, that was not the "big mistake." We had the party in a huge, old, ready-to-be-condemned warehouse right by the freeway. Again, that was not the "big mistake" either. (In fact it was a great and really scary location.)

We had to do all kinds of programming to last the whole night. Like any "great" leader, I delegated much of the responsibilities. I put different leaders in charge of the games. We had a couple parents organize the snacks. We thought it would be fun to show the original *Dracula* sometime in the middle of the night. The leaders would have a chance to rest a bit, and the youth would get a kick out of the old school original. So I used my powers of delegation and gave the assignment of renting the film to one of our adult leaders. He said he would take care of it, and I didn't give it another thought. It was about 2:00 a.m. during the event when that same volunteer turned to me and said, "Oh, by-the-way, I couldn't get the original Dracula movie, but I got another Dracula movie that will work."

I hesitated just a moment, but then just shrugged my shoulders and said, "Cool."

We got everybody seated in one of the warehouse's big rooms and started showing the movie. The leaders were spread out around the room but no one was at the projector once the movie started. I saw no reason to station someone there. We were busy with crowd control and guarding the exits.

About 20 minutes into the movie it goes to a scene of Dracula's castle up in the Transylvania Mountains. It shows clear night with a full moon overlooking a fog-laden valley. The shot is of a fireplace blazing in a huge grand room and then the camera turns to show three women from behind with long dark hair. They are in long, black, flowing gowns, walking slowly and trance-like towards the balcony. The camera moves past them to show the view from the deck and then turns and goes back towards the women. As it approaches the ladies, it is suddenly very clear that their beautiful gowns stop just short of their breasts, and the three of them stand there completely bare-chested in all their glory.

I think every one of the leaders made a mad dash for the projector. You should have heard the noise… The place erupted! You could imagine the junior high boys yelling, "*I LOVE church!!!* Let's come every week!!!" It was chaos for more than a few minutes.

Yes… there were phone calls. And yes… there were visits to parents with full apologies. All because we didn't review a movie before we showed it. Delegating responsibilities is a great thing to do, but it helps to be specific with your expectations.

To this day, I still can't watch *Dracula*.

STORY 13: ICE CREAM FROM HEAVEN
by Alisa Laska

The first few years at my church, I was all about the messy games. I suppose it's a phase that all youth directors go through (and some never get out of). I was all about anything involving whipped cream, gummy worms, and ketchup. I used a messy twister board made of mustard, ketchup, and relish. One time we filled a baby pool with ice water and Swedish fish, and the youth had to use their bare feet to get out any many fish as they could. And who could forget the time that a boy ate so many M&Ms out of ketchup that he got sick?! But not even that incident could stop my messy game madness. Topping it all was our annual "crud war," which ended the year with teens getting salad dressing, chocolate sauce, mustard, and (of course) ketchup all over themselves. (Parents were recruited to spray them off with hoses at the end.)

Looking back on all of it, I'm not sure I can explain my intentions. I wanted youth group to be fun. I wanted the teens to be excited. And I guess I thought that all good youth directors used messy games to accomplish these goals. Our volunteer leaders seemed grossed out by it, but they went along with all of my schemes. A few teens really did not like getting messy, and I think it actually turned them away from youth group. I didn't think much about it at the time, but looking back, this might have been a huge oversight. I'm not sure if the games got anyone to come in the door... but I know it caused a few of them to run out the door.

One of these messy games will go down in history as the worst game I ever did. I got the concept off of a youth ministry idea website. It was called "Ice Cream from Heaven." I thought it sounded perfect. It was two of my favorite things: ice cream and heaven.

In this messy game, the players would stand around outside of the church building with bowls. A leader would then get up on top of the roof with a large container of ice cream and a scoop. The leader would throw the ice cream down at the teens, and they would attempt to catch it in their bowls. Of course, this would be challenging, and it would get on their heads and arms and … well… everywhere. The leader on the roof would also throw down the toppings to make a "sundae" in their bowls. (Or on their heads, and arms, etc.) Sundaes on Sunday, right? Chocolate sauce, strawberry sauce, whipped cream, and cherries would magically fall from heaven, and the youth would have a great time.

DON'T DO THIS

"Strobe-light volleyball. Sounds like a great idea, right? It is... until the ball that you last saw on the other side of the net smacks you in the face. I decided to give this game a try at the very first lock-in that I ever led. We got the strobe going and started playing, but we could never make it past a serve. The ball would either hit the ground or bust someone's lip! I had a teen on the ground bleeding, saying, 'Please, Mr. Ryan, we don't wanna play this game anymore!' To which I replied, 'Come on, you guys, this is fun!' But that 'fun' only lasted until I, myself, got hit in the face. Please don't play this game."

Ryan Sidhom

We handed out the bowls. We didn't have a huge budget, so we took whatever we could get from the kitchen closet. This means we were armed with white styrofoam bowls—the kind sold in packs of 1,000. Our leaders passed them out outside of the church, along with plastic spoons. One of our dedicated volunteers climbed the indoor steps to the top floor of the church, unlocked the special door that goes outside, and climbed onto the roof. Thankfully this particular part of the roof was level, so we didn't have to worry about him falling off.

It was the end of the night, and our group was hungry. They were excited for the ice cream, so as our leader started throwing it down from the roof, they were excitedly running back and forth to catch it. The teens were laughing and doing their best to get their snacks. It looked like it was going to be a fun way to end our event.

The problem occurred when the ice cream hit the bowls and flew straight *through* them, making a hole in each bowl. I stood by, stunned. It had not occurred to me that the ice cream could actually go *through* the bowls. But, sadly it did. The leader on the roof was a trooper and kept trying. Ice cream kept falling (from heaven). But each time, the ice cream careened down at a high rate of speed and made a hole in each and every bowl.

I was starting to get frustrated and so were the youth. I know they just wanted to eat the ice cream. They started running into each other on purpose or sitting on the ground. A couple of them were eating ice cream off the ground. It was going downhill fast.

I didn't see it at the time, but a few of the youth snuck away. The leader on the roof abandoned the idea of getting the ice cream in the bowls and started to just aim for the teens—especially those who were sitting down. Out of nowhere, several of the youth appeared on the roof with him and grabbed the ice cream toppings. They started spraying the toppings all over the place, down onto the other teens and, of course, all over the leaders. The other leaders and I started shouting at them to get down. My heart started racing thinking of all the angry parents this would lead to and even a possible lawsuit if they fell. The youth didn't understand why they had to come off the roof, but were nice enough to come down.

Even after all of this, the dedicated leader on top of the church *still* didn't give up. He grabbed the whipped cream and cherries and started squirting and throwing them down onto the teens. But by this point, we'd all had enough of ice cream from heaven. We called off the game and told everyone to head in and clean up.

It had to have been at least 15 minutes later as we came back outside when we heard a shout from up above. "*Help!* I'm locked out! I'm stuck on the roof!"

The other leaders and I looked at each other in confusion. How could this have happened? That door could only be locked from the inside with a pad lock…

It was then that we spotted the three youth who had made their way up onto the roof earlier. They were smiling and snickering to themselves. I let out a huge sigh and went over to talk to them.

That ice cream was *not* from heaven…
Think through (and maybe even try out) games before you do them. And while I'm not going to say that all messy games are bad, it might be a good idea to do a self-check on *why* you're doing them. I think it's important that we maintain the passion and are willing to try crazy ideas, but I used *unsafe* ideas. We all will have volunteers who are following our lead. I hate to think of how often people have tried my ideas and suffered because I didn't stop and think though the consequences of the game/event/retreat/etc. that I was having them do. Not worth it. Come to think of it, these games probably didn't just cost me a few teens… I bet they cost me a few leaders too.

STORY 14: SCANDALOUS PIZZA
by Len Kageler

I spent most of my full time youth ministry life on the west coast. Teens loved pizza at events, of course. The favorite, by far, was "Hawaiian Pizza" which included Canadian bacon and pineapple. 'Twas a favorite of mine as well.

At my first pizza event in my new church in New Jersey, I couldn't understand why none of the local restaurants had this kind of pizza. "That is so weird," I kept thinking to myself. I finally found a place that would make them specially for me, so I ordered six Hawaiian and two plain.

At the event most of the teens wouldn't even touch Hawaiian and were scandalized by my poor choice. Their displeasure, shall we say, was not subtle. Of the six Hawaiian pizzas present, only one was consumed, and that was mostly by me.

STORY 15: ICE CREAM AND DRUG DEALS
Name Withheld

Like many youth ministries with an outreach focus, we provide transportation for teens whose parents work nights or don't drive, if it's too far for the teens to walk. After youth group, if the weather is warm, we take them out for ice cream on the way home. (We pretend it's a treat just for them. It's really a treat for us adults too of course.)

On one particular warm evening after youth group, we only had three teens with us, so we stopped to get ice cream at one of our favorite places—which, it just so happens, is located next to the local police station (a detail that will come into importance in just a second).

While waiting in line, a man I didn't recognize approached our guys (all of whom were eighth-grade boys). They didn't seem bothered. In fact, it seemed like they knew him. Trying to give them their space and independence, I continued to place our order while they conversed.

As I came back with the ice cream, I heard some muttering from the unknown man, and I caught a glance from my husband that communicated: "We just avoided a disaster." But the look also said, "Don't ask, let's just go." The young man told the boys he would meet up with them later and left.

I drove a little faster than normal to their homes and we said our goodbyes. The last teenager barely finished closing the car door before my curiosity took over, and I yelled "*What on earth happened back there?!*"

My husband shook his head with disappointment, "Drugs."

"WHAT?!" I couldn't believe it! "That man tried to sell our teens drugs?!!?" I could feel the anger begin to bubble up inside of me at the very thought.

"No," he said looking down. "That guy was trying to buy them. Apparently our guys sell them, and he is one of their regular customers..."

My own youth, who I poured into, prayed over, and loved, were about to sell drugs without much (or any) hesitation... in front of their youth director... *right outside of a police station.*

I think that qualifies as a youth ministry failure.

STORY 16: BAD MAGIC
by Jonathan Hobbs

I once saw speaker and writer Mark Matlock do a magic trick where he made it look like he was putting a straw up his nose and then pulling it out of his mouth. I've done a few minor magic tricks in my time, and I was able to see how he was palming the straw when he pushed it up his nose and then pushing it out in front of his mouth. Simple trick. (But giving credit where it's due—Mark does this trick *very* well.)

A few months later, I was on a mission trip putting on a VBS in another city. I was trying to show off with the kids, and I decided to show them a few magic tricks. I did a couple of my normal tricks and when they asked for another, I decided to blow their minds with Mark's "straw up the nose" trick.

One of the most important aspects of the trick is making sure you don't hold the straw too firmly—otherwise it won't slip in your palm. This, sadly, is the mistake I made that day. In front of 20 horrified children, I accidentally jammed a straw up my nose and proceeded to bleed for the next hour.

It's still referenced by my youth. Any time I think I'm cool, they'll simply say, "Hey, Jon… show us that trick with the straw…"

STORY 17: COPS AND CAPTURE THE FLAG
by Jeff Smyth

This was my first *big* youth event in my first full-time youth pastor position. I had been planning this event with my volunteer leaders, parents, and leadership high schoolers. Actually, I had been planning this event even before I was hired. I knew that this event was going to be epic. Possibly the greatest youth ministry event in Canada's history.

There would be two teams. The whole church divided in half, down the middle, using painter's tape. The tape was the recommendation of the custodian. (Quick tip: Never disagree with your church's custodian. Ever.)

I communicated with everyone I could think of who needed to know about this event. The church staff, board, and property committee were all in the loop. Parents were called in as reinforcements. Even the owner of the local coffee shop where I worked on all the details leading up to this event knew about it. He even gave some suggestions! The event started to build a great deal of momentum when the youth were informed that all the lights would be out in the church. This event was going to be the launch of my ministry.

The night arrived, and everyone who was involved was early or on time. Everything was set up and ready to go. The doors opened, and teens started streaming in through the main entrance of the church. As they registered, each participant was given a reflective arm band that was color-specific for their team. They also got a matching glow-stick necklace. Our game referees wore construction vests with the big reflective stripes on them. All the leaders had flashlights and walkie-talkies. Everyone gathered to hear the rules and the obligatory warnings. Each team was then sent to their respective areas and were told the game would begin when the lights went out.

As soon as it went dark you could hear the youth scream with excitement. Then the hoards began stampeding throughout the church. The first game lasted about 45 minutes, and there were only a few minor bumps and bruises that we had to sort out.

We brought the teams together and made some modifications to the rules. During that meeting, I saw a group of our twelfth-grade guys whispering and giving each other secret directions on their hands. I thought to myself, "These guys are right into this. That's pro!"

The teams were sent to their "base" areas for round two and the lights went out. Everyone knew that something special was going to happen—or at least that's what I felt.

(DON'T DO THIS)

"I knew a guy who was on a mission trip to Mexico, and they had a layover somewhere in Texas. One of his teens lagged behind for one reason or another and the youth director decided to go on–leaving the youth behind. The teen missed the flight and got stranded in the airport. They called home and their parents bought them a ticket back. When the youth pastor returned from the trip he was immediately fired. The crazy thing is that he didn't understand why he was being let go. As if leaving a someone's kid in an airport wasn't that big of a deal…"

Brady Rennix

Fifteen minutes in I got a call about a serious injury in the back stairwell. As I rushed to the scene, I made a mental note to have a nurse or a first-aid person on site next time I had an event like this. As I arrived to the stairwell, I saw three teens holding various areas of their bodies, and I thanked God no one was holding their heads.

As I was assessing the injuries, I received another call saying they needed me at the front entrance. I think I rolled my eyes, and then I said calmly into the radio, "I'm dealing with three injuries, so it will have to wait." There was a long pause, and then another call came over the radio. They repeated their message slower to add emphasis to the urgency at the main entrance of the church. I did what any great leader would do: I made a critical decision to stay and care for the injured teens. I also turned my radio off.

After fifteen minutes I walked slowly with my injured youths to the main entrance. Standing there was group of my leaders with the reason I was being called on the radio: four police officers. Now our church was not technically in town, so these were not our local police but our provincial police. This is the Canadian equivalent of America's state police. The important factor is that they had less of a connection to our actual area. They were also far more heavily armed.

Someone from across the road had called the police, because they had seen flashlights on the flat roof of the church. My mind then flashed back to the group of twelfth-grade boys who were making plans. The police officers grilled me. They were not happy. They raked me over the coals for putting on such an unsafe event and letting teens run in the dark. They explained that I was lucky that there were only three injuries. At this point I blanked out, and I only saw the officer's face. At some point round two of the game ended, so the youth began to arrive at the scene. Before leaving, the officers told me in no uncertain terms that we would face a substantial fine if they were called back.

I thanked each of them for their concern, and assured them I understood what they said and would make the appropriate changes for any future events. Apparently my "epic" event had almost crossed some sort of legal line.

My youth don't remember many events we did. They don't remember the Bible studies or the talks. But they remember the cops showing up at their first big youth group event. It's how I learned that people tend to remember the *worst* thing a lot more than they remember the *best* thing. So it's important to make sure to avoid disasters… because it's not what we want youth to remember about our ministry.

STORY 18: FIRE UP THE GRILL

by Jonathan Hobbs

One year on a missions trip I made burgers on the grill. But the church where we were staying only had a charcoal grill. Keep in mind that this before the days where you just googled any and everything. I just figured I was supposed to plop the charcoal in, douse it with lighter fluid, and strike the match.

Well… the fireball was *spectacular.* The youth gasped and applauded, and I tried to play it off as being deliberate. I threw on some frozen burgers, flipped them when each side looked done, threw cheese on top, and put them in a bun. I was amazed at how quickly they cooked! I figured charcoal must be faster than gas… who knew!?

About two minutes later, the first teen barfed. The second one barfed about two minutes after that. If memory serves, there were two more lunches brought back up. And everyone felt sick.

In charcoal grilling, it turns out, one must create a steady heat coming from the coals where the temperature is neither too low nor too high. Too low and the food cooks too slowly and can dry out. Too high and the outside of the food will cook but the inside stays raw. I erred (as you might have guessed) on the side of the latter.

STORY 19: ATHEIST ON MY MISSION TRIP-BAD IDEA?
by Alisa Laska

Right after college I started working for a small church. I had my fancy youth ministry degree and I was ready to take on the world. The church had been saving up for several years for an international mission trip. I was excited because I had been on several mission trips throughout college, and they were life-changing experiences for me. But could I lead a group of youth to a foreign country I'd never been to? Sure! Why not?

We prepared and dreamed about the trip for about a year before we really sat down to decide on a location or mission organization. Walking through the exhibit hall at a youth workers' convention, I saw a mission organization represented that I really admired. I had been on two trips with them in college, and I really respected their philosophy of missions and what they stood for. They told me all about their youth trips, and I took home all of the brochures.

A few days after returning, I talked with our elder, our youth team, and others at the church. I shared my excitement about this organization and all that we'd get to do on the mission trip. They were a little hesitant. This caused me immediate frustration, because of course I, the 22-year-old youth worker, knew what was best for the church. As they looked over the brochures, they said they weren't sure the organization fit well with our church's mission theology.

I didn't understand what they were talking about. Didn't everyone want to go on a mission trip to share the love of Jesus? It turns out that church had very strong leanings on *how* people should share their faith. And I admit that I understood their concerns to a point. But they pushed so hard against certain mission methodologies that it limited our mission trip options. (Mission-related theology and methodologies had not come up in my interview process with the church... a failure on both our parts.)

I felt strongly that this organization would be a good fit for us, so I worked hard and eventually convinced our church leadership to give us the okay to go. I was thrilled! But the struggle came about as I was talking to our trip coordinator from the organization, and she mentioned that everyone going on the trip needed to be a Christian.

This may seem obvious to you... Maybe you'd even assume that all of your church members or youth group members are Christians. Well, I knew that wasn't the case where I was working. And I didn't see that as a bad thing. In fact, I felt like mission trips were a great way for youth "on the fence" to see faith in action and even take a big step in their Christian walk.

DON'T DO THIS

"While speaking to a crowd on the last night of a missions trip, I said, 'Jesus was a historical person. Like George Washington, Abraham Lincoln, and MLK. He's not like Santa Clause...' (Pause) 'I hope you know Santa Clause isn't real. And Jesus isn't like Santa or the Easter bunny.' The youth laughed. Then throughout the talk I was thinking, 'Jeez... what are you kids being disruptive about?' I found out during the leaders meeting afterward that one of the eighth-grade boys still believed in Santa. I felt terrible, but the youth pastor was like, 'Oh, no... Don't feel bad. This is perfect. I've wanted to tell him for years.'"

Scott Smith

But I was young and inexperienced and didn't know how to express all of this to the coordinator on the phone. So I said okay, hung up, and immediately started worrying. I knew there was one girl who we really wanted to go on the trip who would not call herself a Christian. I talked to her parents, who were Jesus followers, and they loved the idea of her going on the trip. In fact, they kind of insisted on it. So I got back on the phone and called our mission coordinator. I was honest and explained the whole situation. She said that she had to think and pray about it and talk to her supervisors. In the end, she decided to let the girl go, because they felt that maybe the mission trip would be a chance for her to find the Lord as well. I was pumped!

The bigger problem came later on as the youth were signing up. One of the boys who wanted to go was filling out the application when he turned to me and said he really didn't know what he believed about God. "Oh no," I thought. "Not another one!" But then he quickly added that he'd just fill out the application and write the essay as if he was a believer.

Now, this may sound horrible, but I promise I had the best of intentions. I told him to go ahead with that plan. I looked right into his eyes and encouraged him to lie on the application.

I just couldn't imagine calling the coordinator back and saying, "Well… we've got another one!" There was no way they would allow it! I really wanted him to go. I was young, and even though it's cliché, I really didn't know any better.

In some ways, it was the best decision I could have made. On the mission trip, he had an amazing experience. A year or so later, he would call this mission trip a major step in his becoming a Christian. Amen! Right? Well… it's not that simple.

At the end of the trip, the organization had us fill out evaluation forms before returning home. One of the questions on it was, "How your faith had changed through the trip?" The boy apparently filled out the form in a bad mood and had written, "I don't believe in God, and I never will."

But of course, I wasn't aware of this until several weeks later. I was doing a debrief with the mission trip coordinator. (That poor woman. I feel so bad for how much I put her through!) She told me about this statement and was very upset. She reminded me (quite sternly) of the reasons they wanted everyone on the trip to be a Christian. My lapse in judgment had come to light. It didn't have any serious repercussions, other than several years later when we were looking to go on another international mission trip, and they wouldn't let us return.

So I'll be honest and say that to this day I don't know how to file this one away. Was it a fail? I had a teen lie on a mission trip application. Pretty sure I shouldn't have done that. But God used it! How amazing is that? God's grace works in spite of our mistakes, or maybe because of them.

STORY 20: PERU TRIP TRIP-UPS
by Megan DeHaven

My church has a partnership with a ministry deep in the jungles of Peru. They had sent a team from our church almost every year for several years. I had been the youth director for some time, and I started to feel some pressure to attempt to take a youth group down. But I saw so much room for error (and flat out disaster), so I insisted that we take a (small) group along with the next adult team. Everyone seemed happy with that compromise. I presented the trip to the youth and parents and three high schoolers ended up committing to the trip! It was perfect. A nice small group. Very manageable.

I purchased the airline tickets based on the tickets that were already purchased for the adults on the team. There were only two airlines that flew in and out of Peru, and they were both owned by the same parent company. I just simply matched up the airline and times.

We did all the normal stuff: weekly meetings, detailed emails to the parents, support letters, financial deadlines, etc. After months of prep, the day arrived.

The "youth" and "adult" groups drove to the airport together. The adults had done this trip multiple times, so I just followed their lead. They told us to print out our boarding passes before we left home. Done. They wanted to get to the airport in plenty of time. Done. They wanted to do curbside check-in. Sure. We boarded the plan for Miami (our layover stop) with no incident.

We found our way to the gate of our next flight, and one of the adults told the youth to go ahead and call their parents now since their cell phones were going to be "pretty much useless in Peru."

Soon the time came to board the plane. The adult group had purchased their tickets long before we did, so they boarded the plane ahead of us. This left my then-boyfriend (now my husband)—who was my co-leader—and myself with the three high school students. And our seats were in the very last group to be called to board.

When the first of our youth handed the airline attendant her ticket, we were informed—after much confusion—that we were at the wrong gate. The airline had an identical flight leaving at the same time out of the international terminal on the complete opposite side of the airport—approximately a mile, by foot. And that was the flight we were supposed to be on. The flight numbers were literally one digit off—no wonder we hadn't noticed. When I asked the airline to call over to hold the plane, they explained that doing so was against airport policy.

Immediately we sent our fastest teen ahead of us to try and hold the plane. Immediately after that, it occurred to me that he shouldn't go alone, so we sent another teen after him. To make matters worse, the first teen's backpack was apparently unzipped, so his belongings were flying out of his backpack as he was running. The second one was trying to pick up all the things as he chased him. The adult team had no idea that we weren't on board. I tried to call them, but their cell phones were already turned off.

We had to get on a tram and then reenter the airport through a different security gate. When we got there, I asked the TSA officer if they had seen two boys ahead of us. They had *not*. Crud. Now we were late for our flight *and* were missing two of the three high schoolers!

So, I ran ahead to try and stop the plane. They closed the door just as

I arrived and refused to let us board. (Apparently it's a federal offence to reopen the door or to try and block it from shutting. Good to know.) After crying my eyes out to the attendant, they switched our tickets to the next flight out—11:30 p.m. the following night.

The two boys finally arrived at the gate. They had been lost on the airport tram system.

My boyfriend had enough sense to suggest that we get hotel rooms for the night, so that we would be rested for the next day's travels. However, he quickly discovered there was only *one* remaining room in all of the Miami area for the night—so we took it, thinking that we could surely get another room once we got to the hotel. What we didn't know was that there was some major convention/event for the WWE (World Wrestling Entertainment) that weekend—hence the lack of room availability.

It was around two in the morning when we arrived at the hotel. I began begging the receptionist for a second room, when suddenly my boyfriend insisted that we all stay together in the room we'd already reserved. I couldn't believe he was even suggesting this! Boys and girls in the same room?! Boyfriend and girlfriend leader in the same room?! *Terrible idea.* Then he quietly and discreetly encouraged me to look around the lobby. We were surrounded by what appeared to be drunkenness, prostitution, and an array of the other finest activities Miami had to offer. I guess I had been a little tunnel-visioned on the way in and missed it. I nodded. One room would be great, thanks.

As you might have guessed, the hotel's level of cleanliness wasn't of the highest standards. Somehow we got to sleep—for a little while at least.

Early the next morning we were awakened by a frantic phone call from the adult team, who had arrived in Lima only to discover that we had never made it onto the plane. We explained the fiasco and that we'd be arriving the next day. We decided that they should go ahead without us into the jungle, and we'd meet up with them there.

So we showered and did a little touring of the city. Our bags had been checked all the way through to Peru, so we only had what was in our backpacks. I felt like it was definitely a justifiable expense, so we took the group shopping on the church credit card. The easiest place to shop was near the beach, and the cheapest options were fluorescent tees and sweats. In other words, we ended up looking like walking billboards for Spring Break Miami.

When we arrived in Lima, our first course of action was to find our luggage that had arrived on our plane the night before. The customer service desk ran a search for our luggage and came up with nothing, but the agent quickly realized the issue: The airport puts all unclaimed luggage into a warehouse after 24 hours. We were now 24 hours and 15 minutes later than when our luggage arrived—just minutes too late...

Again, tears ensued and I was able to get some agents to go to the warehouse to search for our luggage. Only because we had all—adult group and youth group—checked in together at curbside check-in back in the US and were planning to arrive in Peru together, we had paid no attention to whose name was placed on each piece of luggage. That meant that without the adult team and their IDs—long since taken into the jungle with them—we could only access a few pieces of our luggage. (Our clean underwear was sitting just feet away from us in suitcases we could not claim!) It took some more tears (and a hefty tip), but at last they released the luggage to us.

We did finally make it to the Amazon Jungle... two days later than anticipated... and dressed to impress!

STORY 21: A MUSIC FESTIVAL MESS
by Jonathan Hobbs

The month of June brings many things. Summer begins, school ends, and since 1979, it's when tons of Christian music fans flock to the middle of Pennsylvania for a huge festival called "Creation Fest." And when I say huge, I mean *huge*. Every year they draw something like 60,000-80,000 people to the four-day event covering over 100 acres of farmland with tents and campers (and, of course, stages and sound equipment). Christians of all ages and denominations come from all over the country and beyond.

In my sophomore year of college, a small church in New Jersey hired me as their youth director. I was 19-years-old when I started working there, (No. Not a typo.) The youth were really interested in going to Creation Festival that summer. So, two months after I turned 20, I loaded a 15-passenger van full of kids and headed out to the middle of Pennsylvania.

But don't worry—we had adult supervision. There was Derek, who was someone the pastor sent my way. He was even younger than I was and had recently committed some sort of misdemeanor and needed community service hours. I'm not kidding. For the girls we had Lisa, a friend of mine from school.

It would be an understatement to say that I was not prepared for the realities that hit—and kept on hitting—from the moment we got out of the van.

Problem #1: Tents. We didn't have enough of them. No worries, we'd put leaders in the same one. And this would have worked great if Derek hadn't taken it upon himself to give me "alone time" with Lisa, my crush at the time, by sleeping outside—yes, the youth noticed. No nothing happened.

Problem #2: Places to sit, eat, relax. We had no tables, no chairs, no canopies—the idea of bringing that stuff had never even crossed my mind.

Problem #3: Meal prep. I'd planned on the kids bringing cash to buy their own lunches and dinner. This worked like a charm. For breakfast I supplied the milk and I'd planned on the teens supplying the cereal. This also would have worked out great, if only I'd remembered bowls and spoons.

Problem #4: No tarp. Groups that come to the event tend to bring tarps and put them down to mark their space in the arena. This way the people in the group a) know where to meet you in the arena, and b) don't have to sit directly on the ground. Welp… we had to do without.

Problem #5: Rules. Sure I gave them the basics ("don't die," "no drugs," etc.), and after someone asked if they had to check in with me throughout the day, I came up with a check-in system on the spot. But after all that, I failed to give them a curfew. Rookie mistake that I learned the hard way while falling asleep at 1:30 a.m. with kids still missing. (Oh, yes, I slept.)

Every day came with its own problems, but the last night was the biggest screw-up. We decided we were going to have a "grand finale" campfire after the final concert. We found/bought tons of wood and invited the youth group from the campsite next to us, which was great at first. I did the smart thing and showed people how cool it was to spray lighter fluid directly into a campfire. The visitors looked frightened, but I suspected deep down they were really impressed.

The other youth director seemed to think the fireworks we were throwing in the fire were a bad idea. He actually seemed quite peeved. I didn't understand why.

As the festivities ended, I told the group that I didn't want to have to take back anything more than necessary. Translation: "Burn all the trash."

And burn we did. We burned all the wood. We went to other campsites and got their leftover wood and burned that too. It all had a sort of *Lord of the Flies* vibe to it. I thought to myself, "Wow. I'm such an awesome youth leader. These kids are so lucky."

It was getting late and I was in a conversation with Derek and a teen, when a kid named Alan was still adding stuff to the fire. He, in particular, was very excited about my decree that we "burn everything." At some point he started asking about burning different things around the campsite. And when Alan said, "Jon, can I put this can of shaving cream in the fire?" I didn't even blink.

"Go for it," I said with a cocky smile, and went back to my conversation.

I was mid-sentence when it happened. It was one of the loudest noises I had ever heard. There was a trail of shaving cream from the fire about 25 yards long leading to the back tire of the RV in the campground next to us—the one that had the youth director who had questioned my leadership choices involving campfires and fireworks. The can was now lying on the ground, blackened from the fire with the bottom completely blown out. The rim of the RV was dented. Imagine if it had hit a person...

The youth director next door came out of the RV screaming at the top of his lungs. Something about how his group needed to sleep and how there was no way fireworks that loud were legal to use at the festival.

As I was calming him down, I remember thinking, "I need to just tell the truth and confess my stupidity." So I took a deep breath, looked him in the eye… and lied my butt off.

I'm not proud of it. I was just so scared. I knew what had happened was completely my fault. I told him that we were burning a bag of trash (kind of true) and didn't realize that there was a can of shaving cream in the bag (total lie). I also apologized profusely and told him how awful I felt (totally true). I also told him I'd pay for any damages to the RV (kind of a lie).

It's been over 15 years since that night. I am still in contact with a few of those former high schoolers (mainly thanks to social media), and when the story of the shaving cream can comes up, I still can't laugh. I can't believe I was so stupid.

Think through your retreats *before* going on them. Remember to pack a first aid kit—always. Have faith that warning labels—especially those on cans of shaving cream—mean something. But most of all, know that it's not that important for you to *impress* your youth— definitely not important enough to cause people to get hurt (or worse). Your ministry is about Christ—not about you.

Epilogue: *The following year I took my group back to Creation Fest and one of my high schoolers faked a demon possession in the festival's prayer tent and single-handedly shut it down. To this day he claims he was just having a coughing fit. He just recently graduated from seminary.*

STORY 22: CAPRI SUNS AND PUPPIES [10]
by Allison Blanchet

Years ago I was working for two Catholic parishes on a resort island. After Monsignor Gregory of Mustard Seed Communities spoke at all our Masses one weekend, I asked my middle school class what they thought about his mission helping children in developing countries. My hope was that they would want to help. The conversation went something like this:

"So, who heard Msgr. Gregory at Mass this weekend?"

I'm greeted by a chorus of, "I didn't go to Mass this weekend."

(Insert tangent of, "I know you're in sixth grade, but you need to remind your parents how important it is to take you to Mass on Sunday or Saturday night if your soccer coaches are heathens who don't observe the Sabbath." I'm sure you have a similar script in your pocket.)

"Well, if you didn't hear Msgr. Gregory for yourself, he talked about the children that his mission takes care of in Jamaica, the Dominican

10. Originally published on the blog www.teamcatholic.blogspot.com and in the book *Edge Core Handbook: Tools to Thrive in Catholic Middle School Ministry* edited by Natalie Tansill and Amanda Grubbs, p. 72-74. Used by permission of Life Teen, 2013. Check out www.lifeteen.com for more information.

Republic, Nicaragua, and Zimbabwe who don't have enough to eat.

There's a program where we can support them called Sustain a Life. Wouldn't that be a nice thing for us to do?"

Mikey, a sixth grader, excitedly raises his hand and waves it frantically around. He's such a compassionate child; I knew he'd be the first to want to help. Not even waiting for me to call on him, Mikey blurts out, "Miss Alison! You know how you can buy a star? We could *buy* a poor *kid!*"

This idea is met with great excitement. Nicole, a seventh grader, chimes in, "Yeah! We could keep it here in the youth room. They could sleep on the couch, and you could be its *mom!*"

This is not going in the direction I had hoped, but thinking it was still salvageable, I try to bring them back to the reality of the situation, asking, "Well, that's really nice of you guys to want to take care of a kid, but don't you think they'd miss their family, living in the youth room?"

The youth stare at me, blankly. "No," they all say. "They could play the Wii."

I persist, although I can feel my teeth starting to grind. These young people *will* learn the richness of Catholic Social Teaching and the principle of subsidiarity! So I ask, "You wouldn't want to leave your family and live in the youth room, would you? Even if you had cool stuff, wouldn't you miss them?"

Again, a blank stare and a chorus of, "No."

Still, I am prepared with a plan of action. A way for them to put their faith into motion and sacrifice for others that I am convinced will stir their hearts to serve the common good. "Well, guys, we can't keep a kid here." (This is met with a round of disappointed sighs.) "But we can send them money each month to help feed the kids in Zimbabwe! Isn't that cool? What about if, for the next month, instead of drinking

Capri Suns, we drink water and send the money to feed a child in Zimbabwe?"

"You mean bottled water?" they ask.

"No, that still costs money. I'd give you a cup and you could get water from the water fountain," I explain.

This is met with looks of incredulity and a round of, "No, I don't think so..." At this point, I'm rapidly losing faith in humanity and, specifically, the sixth grade. Hands on my hips, I sternly ask, "You guys, when you die and Jesus asks you how you took care of each other, don't you want to say that you gave up Capri Suns so that kids in Zimbabwe could eat?"

"Well, maybe if we could have hot chocolate instead?" Nicole suggests.

Then, Mikey (Mr. "Buy a Kid!") remembers something. "Miss Alison! You can sponsor a puppy for $15 a month! And they send you a hoodie and a tote bag! That's even cheaper! Could we keep a puppy in the youth room?"

I sigh. "You know what, guys, let's just put in a movie."

As exasperating as this was, it is exactly what I love about middle schoolers. Their minds and hearts are so open, and conversations range from inspiring to completely absurd. We can't run from this critical moment in Christian formation—when ideas are being tested and virtue formed—just because it's a little chaotic and full of dizzying logic. Investing in the lives of middle schoolers is essential. When we meet young people here, forming relationships over puppy dogs and Capri Suns, we help establish a relationship with the Church that they can lean into as they mature into adults.

STORY 23: GIRLS NIGHT OUT
by Megan DeHaven

Many years ago we started an annual tradition of doing a "Night Out" with the youth. The guys have a "Guys' Night Out" and the girls have a "Girls' Night Out." It has become one of the biggest dates on our youth ministry calendar. People dress up. Teens clear their schedules. We've had great success with it. It's a fantastic event to bring all the sixth- through twelfth-grade youth together and do something really special. It's always such a great evening!

Except for one year… One year the girls' night was not an epic success. It was an absolute disaster.

Each year the activity for the night out is different. I had asked around and someone told me about this great dinner theater downtown. It sounded *perfect*. But I'm semi-paranoid about taking kids to a theater. I know that things can sometimes get a little "raw" and I didn't want to expose the girls to that. So I did my homework. I searched the internet. Great reviews! The theater's website spoke in multiple places about the "welcoming family-friendly atmosphere." But in true theater-paranoia form, I called the place to double-check. I explained who we were and what I was looking for. The nice lady who answered the phone assured me that it would be a wonderful evening. It was a three-act play and the meal was served one course at a time in-between the acts. I believe she, too, used the term "family friendly." And on top of this—since I was bringing a "group"—I got to play a small (one line) role in the play!

I asked about the play's storyline for our specific night's performance. It was based on a couple hosting a comical dinner party with their neighbors. Sounded good to me. I made the reservations with the nice lady.

So the night came and the girls dressed to the nines. Parking downtown wasn't cheap, but we had just enough left on the church's credit card to cover the cost. We arrived at the theater in plenty of time, appetizers were served downstairs, and then we were shown our seats.

ACT 1

My first misunderstanding of the evening was immediately apparent. The couple hosting the dinner party on stage had gender-neutral names. It never occurred to me that the couple might be same gender. And this wasn't just same gender… it was a very flamboyantly gay couple. And the actors were milking their roles for every laugh they could get.

This also might be the right time to mention that our church had recently split off from our denomination due to our conservative stance on the definition of marriage. So this added a bit more uneasiness to a situation that was already slightly awkward. However, it was far more the jokes they were telling that made the moment one from which I wanted to escape. I didn't want to bring my youth group to a play where *any* couple was joking this much about their sex life (same sex or not).

Questioning glances were exchanged between the leaders, but I stayed calm. It was a great opportunity. I won't ever pretend that everyone in the world holds the same beliefs as our church. We have to be okay with reality! Our group could enjoy a play even if the main characters were doing something our church did not support. Right? Of course right! And besides… we'd barely eaten since the acts were in between courses. So we stayed. Plus, we figured it couldn't really get any worse.

The curtain closed and the second course came along.

ACT 2

The innuendos got a little more pronounced. The jokes became a little less appropriate. I attempted to respectfully distract the girls with conversation about the food, the décor, anything to distract from the spectacle in front of us. And then a police officer came to the door. But of course, it wasn't really a police officer... it was a female stripper dressed as one. I've never prayed harder for Jesus Christ to return... immediately.

Curtain. I would have actually left and taken the group elsewhere, but I was reminded that we had no money left on the credit card. We spent the budget getting here, and we still hadn't eaten our dinner!

The main course was finally served. Thank goodness the food was so good. I was enjoying my spaghetti and meatballs, when I was reminded by a staff person that I would be on stage for part of the final act. Oh no... the girls were not only going to tell their parents that the play was wildly inappropriate, they were also going to tell them that I was *in* the play. But surely it couldn't actually get *worse*....
Right?

ACT 3

It got worse. I'm not going to go into details, but a blow-up sex doll was involved. I wanted to die. I delivered my line and got off stage as fast as possible. What I wanted to do was stand on my chair and scream, "*What kind of families do you people have that this is considered family friendly?!? Are you insane???*"

But if I had done that I would have missed dessert... and that would have been a shame.

In all honesty, it probably wasn't quite as bad as my memory suggests—or maybe it was—but I remember being so overwhelmed with the feeling of things crashing down around me, it was like a disaster in slow motion. I felt out of control. I was just imagining all the calls I was going to get about it. (By the way, I didn't get a single one.) The girls saw the shock on my face and knew that it wasn't what we had expected. It was raw exposure to secular culture at its finest.

Not sure I have a direct "lesson" to share from this experience... But I'll try. Maybe... 1) always have a backup plan, just in case; 2) make sure you save enough budget for that backup plan; and 3) when someone says "family friendly" you should ask exactly what kind of family they have in mind.

SECTION II: REFLECTIONS

Anna Walters @annaelizya   May 27
Just confidently called a kid Charlie... his name was
Joey. #youthministryfail

Reading the stories in this section brought up many personal emotions for us both. Between the two of us we have 60 years of youth ministry experience, either paid or volunteer. We saw ourselves here again and again. It made us grateful to God that in none of these stories is a young person killed, lost permanently, maimed for life, or driven from the gospel because of the mistakes of some sincere, dedicated, and well-intentioned youth workers.

It's interesting to us that mistakes in this section seem to group themselves into categories. What can we learn from the confessions before us here?

The first two stories ultimately are about the youth worker not thinking about the point of view of the young person. We both laughed out loud in amazement when we first read Marko's story of gamely proceeding with the lesson plan even though his youth could see out the window the fire engulfing homes not far from the church and many were suffering the trauma of evacuation—one an actual home loss.

Some stories made us both feel great, and perhaps you felt the same way: "At least I'm not *that* stupid!"

From Len...
Appreciating the adolescent point of view or adolescent life-world (sociologist love the term "life-world") has become more natural to us. For example, I was sitting behind Samantha, a seventh-grade girl sitting in a circle with 20 other middle schoolers while the youth pastor gave his lesson. She turned around and with a smile on her face

and uncharacteristicly dreamy look in her eyes said to me, "Jordan is so cute!!!"

I noted she was sitting directly opposite eighth-grade boy Jordan, and apparently her life-world in the last 15 minutes was completely focused on longingly gazing at his wonderfulness. I smiled at Samantha, and whispered, "I'm not a very good judge of male cuteness, Samantha, but I'll take your word for it."

What? You might think I should have said, "Sam, you pagan! Don't you realize your youth pastor is teaching God's word? You'd better listen to him!" But I instantly remembered my dominant concern in middle school youth group for three years was Shelly. Could I sit next to her in youth group? Or, better yet, in the van? (Because then our arms might touch!) I wasn't rebellious or anything, but I had Shelley on my mind virtually 100% of the time I was in youth group. I knew that Samantha would mature and the Word would eventually mean as much or more to her than Jordan or his friends.

From Jonathan...

I struggle with appreciating adolescent life-world all the time. In the next section, I have a story (see Story 25) where I go into detail about one such incident. And, recently, I have been convicted by the realization that I've been a bit unfair in my views of some teenagers' life-worlds.

For example, I talk about teenagers' busy schedules like they are the devil. When I hear about another soccer game that's during youth group, or a theatrical production that means a teen can't come to small group, or even just how much homework some of my youth have, I gripe and complain about how life "used to be" and how the teenagers today are "just too busy doing _____." Perhaps you've been there too?

But here we must stop and realize what we're doing. We are upset because the adolescent life-world isn't colliding with our programs the way we think it should. And the proof is simple: We never complain about teens' busy schedules if they are busy with youth group activities. It might do us some good to remember the idea of incarnational. Jesus came into our world. He came to us. We are called to go to them. We need to stop getting upset that they aren't coming to us.

We notice that still other stories in this section were about youth group events that didn't turn out as expected. Poor Tic in "Stop the Movie!" (Story 12), who had to lunge to turn off the video player as R-rated content came on. Our hearts sank, as yours probably did too, over Megan's "Girls' Night Out." It looked as though she made Herculean efforts to make sure the content of the dinner theater would be in the ballpark of appropriate for her girls. And despite her due diligence, she was burned. She is a good example of one who genuinely tried to think things through in advance, but rather than resting in her perfectly acceptable justifications for the disaster, she still found something to learn in that experience and to share with others: Always have a Plan B and know that there are emergency monies available if one has to pivot 180 degrees from the plan, get out of a situation or event, and go do something else.

A larger scale of youth ministry experience than the one-evening event is the youth group trip. Early in our ministries we just assumed teens would behave as expected as Christian young people, and that while accidents and unexpected things happened perhaps to others, those things certainly would not happen to us and in our ministries. How wrong we were! We now assume, and encourage other youth workers to also assume, that something unexpected will happen. The unexpected might turn out to be funny. Len was once Christmas caroling with 25 high school students on the unfortunately nicknamed "porno-row" (no kidding!) in a nearby city center's worst neighborhood, when the owner of a strip club came out, thanked us, and gave our youth choir director (age 16) a Christmas stocking. Rebekah, our director, thanked the lady, and we gathered around to get the candy that we assumed was in the stocking. It wasn't candy in there, however, rather flavored condoms, handcuffs, and other sex toys.

The unexpected may, on the other hand, turn out stressful and possibly deadly… like when Len led a rafting trip, and one of the rafts flipped and went under a logjam. (He learned the hard way that he had no business leading a raft trip down a wild glacier-fed river!)

We both now encourage youth workers to talk through the details of any trip with others, especially with those who are quiet, or even negative. These individuals will think of what might go wrong more easily than some of us would on our own. If we ourselves are not particularly discerning, detail-oriented, or safety-conscious, we need people around us who will think about worst-case scenarios and help us to be ready.

Working with youth directly—teaching them, having events and trips with them, just being with them—are what most of us *love* about youth work. However, the stories in this section show us the need to guard our hearts, use our heads, and be ready for the unexpected.

Questions for Reflection or Discussion

1. If you had to pick the most relatable story in this section, which one would it be and why? Which did you find the most shocking and why?

2. Some of these stories show a deep love of being with youth. What do you most enjoy about being with young people?

3. Some might argue that while planning is important, we needn't get too stressed about details because, after all, God is in control and he will take care of us. What do you think about that response? What do you think the parents of your youth think about that idea?

4. Have you ever made a working-with-youth-directly kind of mistake that was so potentially catastrophic, you now thank God for his mercy and grace? If so, take some time right now to again thank him for his mercy and grace. If you, on the other hand, have made a mistake that caused real harm and suffering

to any youth or their families, have you done everything possible to make amends? If there is nothing more you can do, are you fully convinced of God's forgiveness? Find a trusted person with whom you can discuss this.

Major Project Ideas for the Classroom

1. Read the book *Better Safe than Sued* by Les Christie[11] and write a book review that youth ministry volunteers would find helpful.

2. Interview five full-time youth workers on the subject of "The Unexpected." Write a five-page paper discussing what they learned from their own experiences of dealing with the unexpected in youth ministry.

3. Go to Amazon.com, enter "dealing with the unexpected" and you will find page after page of books dealing with this topic in many areas of life. Choose five of these books to obtain, prepare a 60-minute seminar for youth workers outlining first general principles about dealing with the unexpected; second, specific applications to youth ministry (from your interviews, this book, and your own experience); and third, Bible passages that connect to the topic with an emphasis on God's presence, hope, and power.

---

11. Christie, Les. *Better Safe than Sued: Keeping Your Students and Ministry Alive* (Grand Rapids: Zondervan/Youth Specialties, 2009).

"Success isn't permanent and failure isn't fatal."

Mike Ditka

"Success consists of going from failure to failure without loss of enthusiasm."

Winston Churchill

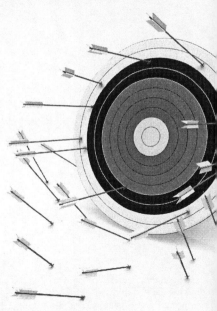

SECTION III
FAILURES WITH PARENTS AND VOLUNTEERS

mistakes made working with parents of youth
and/or ministry volunteers

SECTION III: INTRODUCTION

"Of course we lie to parents! They ask if the mission trip
will be safe, and we look right in their eyes and say, 'Yes!' "
Mike Yaconelli

If somewhere in your past you were taught how to enfold, encourage,
equip, and unleash youth ministry volunteers, you are among the
few. Unfortunately, even some who were taught it in a class or read it
in a book may not have realized how important it would be in actual
real-world youth ministry. The same goes for enfolding, encouraging,
equipping, and unleashing parents. But these skills are important for
those who value being employed in church-based or parachurch
based youth ministry.

Most stories in this section are not very lighthearted. You may be able
to chuckle with Amy as you read how she blissfully thought she could
single-handedly cook spaghetti for 200 and put the water (5 gallons
worth) on to boil 20 minutes prior to dinner being served. Most of
these stories, however, are sobering and can help us all understand
some of the dynamics that are normally part of ministry.

For both of us, failure with volunteers and/or parents forced us to pay
attention to these previously ignored aspects of youth ministry. We
were, like some of the authors in this section, initially chagrined by
the realization that the youth worker has to think beyond the young
people themselves to have a ministry that flourishes.

STORY 24: LEFT BEHIND
by Ron Belsterling

Have you ever returned from a youth group trip *without* one of
the teens who went? Without the parents knowing about it? And,
intentionally? That's what I did. And surprisingly enough, I was a
fairly seasoned vet when I did this.

We took the youth group to visit a Christian college. It was a fun
weekend trip and gave the high schoolers a chance to see what it
would be like to attend a place like that after graduation. As we were
getting ready to leave for home, one of the boys informed me that
he was staying with his brother, who was attending the school. I
explained that he could not stay behind because his parents did not
inform me that he was staying, but he persisted and said that he and
his parents had discussed it and that they were fine with it. They
wanted their boys to take advantage of an opportunity for "brotherly
bonding." He was selling it hard, but I wasn't buying it. Not for a
second.

Unfortunately, it wasn't that simple. I was in the awkward space where
what he was saying *could have* been true. To complicate matters, the
boy's father had recently expressed frustration about me not trusting
his son enough. I tried calling the parents. There was no answer at
home, which was the only number to call since this was in the age
before cell phones. The boy emphatically assured me it had been
planned and approved by his parents. He explained that his father

was making a business trip coming through that exact town in the next few days and would pick him up then. He was adamant and convincing. And his father's "pep talk" to me about trust was echoing in the back of my mind. It all made for a perfect storm. I second-guessed, and eventually ignored, my instinct and better judgment.

So, I left him. And at first all seemed fine. His parents were not at the church to pick him up. In fact, they didn't call that evening either. I went to bed without any anxiety. And then the phone rang at midnight.

It was the boy's mother saying she had waited for our return, trying to be as patient as possible. Since it was so late and her son had not yet come home, she'd decided to call my wife to see if all was okay—but, to her great surprise, I had answered the phone instead. She wanted to know where her son was. I explained then, with great trepidation, that he was still at the college. She did remain polite, but expressed "confusion" as to why on earth I would have left him there.

I had an immediate rush of panic that took me from being half asleep to being very much awake. In a single breath I told her that her son told me he had her permission to stay *and* that I'd tried to call but could not reach her or her husband. (I also began to search the deep recesses of my mind for any conversations I'd recently had about job openings in other churches.)

At this point it was obvious she had not given him any such permission. This young man clearly lied. Big time. I clearly was an idiot. Big time. Later, her husband called and clearly expressed *his* "confusion" (not so politely) and reinforced my own conclusion that I'd been an idiot.

I did learn lessons from that experience.
- Do not return from a youth group trip one person short. I sometimes think back and wonder if having done so intentionally was worse than doing it accidentally. (Though accidentally would not have been good either.)

- Do not believe a young person's story, no matter how good it sounds, if believing it requires you to put their safety, your job, and own family's security in jeopardy.

- Do not veer from plans that have been communicated to parents, unless the change can be discussed with them or they were warned of such possibilities ahead of time.

By the grace of God (and the senior pastor), I did keep my job. (And, yes, that young man did lie to me again. And I did not believe him when he did.) I learned an important lesson about discernment, trusting my own judgment, and not being naïve. I no longer let anyone talk me out of what I know to be the only right possible decision. If I'm going to make a mistake when a young person's safety is an issue, I'd rather make it because I erred on the side of caution. Proverbs 8:5, "O naive ones, understand prudence; And, O fools, understand wisdom" (NASB).

STORY 25: CORRECTION VIA SOCIAL MEDIA
by Jonathan Hobbs

Dan started attending our youth group because of a friend (a *female* friend) who was one of our regular attendees. He asked her out, but she had no desire for a relationship. So, not long after that he became friends with a few of the youth group girls and asked one of them out, but she also turned him down. A few weeks later, he asked a *third* girl out: Sarah. And Sarah was all about it.

To Dan's credit, the boy became a regular attendee on Sunday nights, and even came to our Sunday morning services! He participated in all the events and retreats, and even signed up for the mission trip. He would regularly quote Scripture in his Facebook status. The truth is, I didn't know if it was for real or if he was faking, but if he *wasn't* being real, he was definitely faking it well.

Not surprisingly, there were a few issues with Dan and Sarah committing a little PDA (Public Display of Affection). They weren't overt… nothing like heavy making out. They cuddled a lot, always sat near one another, etc.

At first, the couple seemed to be open to me talking to them about it and asking them to "bring it down a notch." But after a while they started getting defensive. I probably could have addressed it in a better way, but eventually I just decided to let it go. (I even felt that my talking about it was making it worse.)

The boy's parents were not members of our church, nor did they attend anywhere else. In fact, I think it would be accurate to say that they were actually slightly "anti-church." They weren't atheists, but they seemed to be very suspicious of organized religion. (For example: They didn't really get the idea of "youth group" and especially questioned why a grown man would want to hang out with teenagers. They were particularly weirded out when I invited their son to coffee.) But after an initial meeting with the parents, where I explained our program and its goals, all seemed to be well.

Back to Dan and Sarah. People at youth group grew increasingly uncomfortable around the happy couple… and not surprisingly the two of them slowly stopped coming to youth group. (Which, of course, really annoyed me. It's exactly what I was worried about and warned them would happen.)

A few weeks later, during a day off, my wife asked me to do a minor home repair project… or at least it was supposed to be minor. It wasn't. This raised my blood pressure and frustration levels. During a quick break from the work, I decided to check my Facebook. Right at the top of my news feed was a status update from Dan, and this time it wasn't Scripture. It said something like, "I don't think there's really such a thing as PDA. It's just people's opinions and it's all just bulls---."

Maybe it was because I was exhausted and frustrated. Maybe it was because he used the term PDA, and that was a trigger word for me. Maybe it was just because I was tired of the whole ordeal. But for whatever reason, I decided to do the stupidest thing you can on social media: I tried to make a logical argument.

I don't remember exactly what I said in my comment, but it was something like, "Dan, you know that's not true. And if your actions make people uncomfortable you should have the maturity to stop and respect other people's wishes. There are also rules that you have to follow… in school… in public… in youth group… etc. Come on, man… be real."

He responded. I responded back.

I tried to back-peddle at one point and even said something like, "Listen… this probably isn't something to talk about over Facebook. I'll gladly treat you to lunch or coffee and we can talk about it then. Let me know if you're interested."

And then the call came.

I thought it was Dan calling me. Nope. It was his father—and he wasn't happy.

I sat there and listened to Dan's dad scream at me for "sticking my nose into something that wasn't my business." He told me to stop talking to his son about relationships—that I should (direct quote) "just stick to teaching him stuff that's in the Bible." He said only a creep keeps inviting teenage boys out to coffee or lunch. He even quoted me from our first conversation and told me that I was going back on what I'd told him youth group was about.

It was about a 15-minute conversation, and it left me angry, upset, and even questioning if I should start looking into a new career. My wife tried to talk to me and calm me down, but I was too amped up to think straight. I called Sarah and told her about the conversation. I'm not even sure why. I guess I thought I somehow was hurting their relationship, and I wanted to apologize. I don't remember what I said. In fact, I don't even remember calling her (my wife reminded me that I did that). I emailed my senior pastor (perfect thing to do when you're amped and can't think straight) to let him know about the conversation. Dan's dad was upset enough that he might have

DON'T DO THIS

"We were on a mission trip with a first-time leader who'd been interviewed and had a clean background check. He was driving us to the worksite, but apparently our car's taillight was broken. So a police officer pulled us over. He checked the leader's license, but then suddenly asked him to step out of the car. That's when the handcuffs came out. It turned out there was a warrant out for his arrest–something to do with fraud, I believe. But the background check had been clear! (We went back and checked again just to be sure.) So… we told the youth that he had to go take care of some personal stuff."

Name Withheld

contacted the church to complain, so I didn't want the senior pastor having any surprises. I also deleted the comments I made on Dan's Facebook status.

The crazy thing is, Dan didn't stop coming to youth group. Heck—he even signed up for the day trip to the beach a couple weeks later. (Even though Sarah wasn't coming!) But the father and I never talked again. The mother communicated with me a couple of times, and when I tried to address what happened on that day, she stopped me and said it was something I had to take up with Dan's father. She was staying out of it.

In retrospect, I *know* the things the father said to me on the phone were wrong. He was angry with me. I'm also relatively certain he thought I was some kind of pedophile and was after his son. We disagreed about what was appropriate behavior, and it was clear he thought I was a terrible person for trying to correct his son's actions.

But here's what God put on my heart: *Dan's dad had the right to feel that way.*

I cannot speak for all youth directors, but in my experience, so many of us have built our ministries around only those people who (at least kind of) get the idea of youth ministry. We assume that people understand the idea of spiritual mentoring. We assume that the idea of grown adults choosing to hang out with teenagers makes sense to the parents of our youth. I think it's healthy for us to occasionally remember that our job descriptions look incredibly odd to anyone outside of the church.

We have a system of doing things—which in itself isn't a bad thing, but these systems tend to only work for people that fit a certain mold. And we are so entrenched in this that we are completely unequipped to handle people that don't fit into that mold. Call me crazy, but I don't see that as a good place to be. I know that it wasn't a good place for me to be.

I also learned—or at least was reminded—that social media is not the place to try and correct people. No one looks intelligent arguing online. No matter the content, social media is not the place to have a pastoral conversation. It's simply not helpful. It's not helpful when parents try to correct their kids publicly online. It's not helpful when friends try to correct friends online. It's *really* not helpful when youth pastors try to correct teenagers online. No matter how wrong the young person is, the youth pastor never comes out the other end looking good. It's not very wise. It's not usually very helpful. Most importantly, it's not usually very Christlike.

STORY 26: WHEN TO COMMUNICATE
by Alisa Laska

I think every youth worker has made the mistake of getting a little caught up in some of the teen drama that happens in our groups. Or maybe I'm just saying that to make myself feel better. But where two or more teens are gathered, there is drama (pretty sure that's biblical). Most of the time it's minor stuff. Two girls liking the same boy. One guy likes his friend's sister. This girl was rude to this girl and now they're not speaking. The list goes on. But sometimes the drama goes up a few notches. This happened to me, and to this day I'm left wondering if I made the right call.

The details are not overly important and are also technically confidential, but basically one boy in the group did something with his friend's sister. I don't know exactly what "something" was, but it was more than nothing. And I'm relatively sure it was less than everything.

I dove into the mess with the purest of intentions. I wanted to make sure everyone was reconciled back to the group. I wanted harmony. I wanted family.

Things went back and forth… this one didn't want to come to youth group anymore, especially if *that one* was coming, etc. Finally, things were starting to look settled. But all year long, this situation weighed on my heart. I was upset that two in our group were making bad choices together. I was upset that the brother was not willing to talk to me about it and stopped coming to youth group. I also really wrestled with whether or not to tell their parents about the incident. My first thought was that they would really want to know about this and would want to punish the teens for their behavior. This literally kept me awake at night. Both of the boys involved asked me to keep everything confidential. I didn't want them to feel like if they told me anything, I'd just run and tell their parents.

In a previous youth group, I had told a parent something that happened with their child and when the teen found out about it, she got very angry, refused to come to youth group, and spread the word to all of her friends. I was not eager to repeat that.

Since I was unsure of what to do, I talked with two people who have a lot of experience with confidentiality. I spoke with a woman who worked with the county on sexual violence and educating teenagers. She asked if the situation was forced on the girl. She asked if she was okay, and I relayed that I believed she was. After hearing about the situation, the woman agreed that it would be best to keep it confidential.

DON'T DO THIS

Shortly after I was hired, a few parents told me very bluntly they had wanted the church to hire the other candidate that they had interviewed. They formed a committee to try to get me to resign. One of the parents called to tell me this was happening—but not trying to be helpful. She was rubbing my nose in it. The conversation was getting heated, and I hung up on her. I called the senior pastor to let him know what happened. He answered the phone even though he was in a meeting with the local head of our denomination. He had just been informed that the church was asking him to resign. It's a shame. He was one of the few people I had supporting me. I'm still here, but I'm guessing not for long.

Name Withheld

I also talked with a professional pastoral counselor about the situation. She also felt that I should keep it confidential. We didn't feel that it was a situation where someone was harming themselves or others, such as a suicidal person, so she felt that it was important that the youth be able to talk to me confidentially. She felt that sneaking out of the house and hooking up was a common teenage behavior and not necessarily something to be overly alarmed about. After talking with both women, I decided to hold the situation in confidence.

Mid-year, it seemed that things were resolved for the most part and everyone had moved on. As summer began and we were preparing for our annual mission trip, the girl's mom talked to me briefly and said that her son had told her about… well… everything, including that he had confided in me about the situation that happened back in the fall. She asked me to watch her daughter and "that boy" on the trip, because they didn't seem to be a good influence on each other. She then added, "This is really not a great time to talk about it, but we'd like to have a meeting with you sometime about all of this." Immediately my heart started racing, and I got very anxious.

Since the mission trip was that week, I didn't get a chance to talk with her further. I didn't see the two youth together at all during the week except for sitting next to each other on the ride home.

The rest of the summer was very busy for both their family and then mine. I kept waiting for that phone call from her to set up a meeting, but it never came. My anxiety levels were very high. Given that this had kept me up many nights already and now she seemed pretty upset, I kept thinking of the worst-case scenarios. Was she going to tell our pastor and try to get me fired?

Toward the end of the summer, I talked with my spiritual director about it. She encouraged me not to feel anxious, but to feel confident in the decision I had made. She also encouraged me to step out and call the parent myself. At first I was thinking that I'd never do that, but the more I thought about it, the better the idea sounded.

That September, I decided I'd delayed long enough. I took the step and called the parent. She said that yes, she had been very angry when she found out that I knew about the situation and hadn't told her. She was able to share her legitimate concerns about her daughter, and I was able to share with her why I had chosen to keep confidentiality.

At first she still seemed upset and felt that they had needed to know. As we talked, however, her mother began to understand my perspective a little more, and I began to understand hers. At the end of the conversation, we each apologized for the situation, and I said that it had felt really good to talk about it because it really had kept me up at night. She said she was glad that I called.

I learned that some decisions in ministry are really tough and there won't be a clear answer. All we can do is weigh both sides, seek the trusted advice of others, and make the decision we believe is in the best interest of the youth involved. But, most importantly, I was reminded that parents want to be heard and communicated with. I'm still not sure if I made the right decision or not during all the drama, but I *do* know that I made the right decision to call and talk to the parent directly. Opening that line of communication did so much to begin to repair the relationship. I learned that parents want to know all they can about their kids. They want to know the good, the bad, and the ugly, because in the end they just want to keep them safe. They trust us to do the best we can for their kids, keeping them safe and growing toward Christ.

STORY 27: PARENTS (SIGH)
by Jeff Smyth

Years ago I was approached by a youth group mom who wanted to start a meeting for parents to get together for prayer, support, and sharing ideas. I asked for clarity on what expectations she had for this group. She basically just restated that they would get together for prayer, support, and ideas. I agreed to help her get things running. After all, having parents praying is not a bad thing. Having parents supporting one another is not a bad thing. Having parents share ideas is not a bad thing.

But… there was… something…

A tiny feeling in my gut left me a little unsettled. Was this a bad idea? Or was that just my lunch? I started to over think this whole thing. Eventually I began envisioning a mob of parents with pitchforks outside my office door. That might not make any sense, but that is where my mind went. Pitchforks. I was getting nervous at the possibility that I was developing the gift of prophecy… and this was all going to end very poorly.

We decided the parents' group would start meeting after our Sunday evening service, which was going to kick off in a few weeks. It made sense to have them launch at the same time. But as we came closer to the date, I was growing more and more apprehensive about the whole thing. I booked a room for them to meet in and even communicated with all our parents about the meeting. I felt like I had helped out and done my part, but my uneasiness grew and grew. I started calling this parent just to confirm she was excited about the meeting, which she was. Of course she was. A parental coup (with pitchforks) was about to begin, and I didn't have the courage to stop it.

The fateful day came. Our evening service was about to start, and I had scheduled a well-known youth speaker to come and join us that night. The numbers were higher than expected, which was nice but also put me a little on edge. Just before the service was about to get going, the husband of the youth group mom came up and reminded me to announce the parents' gathering afterwards. I didn't roll my eyes… but I really wanted to.

I went up on stage and welcomed everyone, shared some upcoming information that was church related and then welcomed our speaker. I didn't announce the parents' gathering. The speaker did a great job talking about teen issues, and he was well received. I went up to close the service, and right before I prayed I said, "If any of the parents here tonight are interested, tonight we are starting a group for prayer, support, and sharing ideas." I told them the meeting time and the room number. I did my part. But instead of feeling like Jesus (the suffering servant), I felt more like Pontius Pilate (washing my hands of the matter). I announced it more like an afterthought.

Then it began to spiral out of control. Within minutes of the service ending, this lovely mother hurried up to me at the front of the auditorium and said the room the group was to meet in was locked. I told her that I had booked the room, and I gave her my keys to open the door. She said it was too late, and she began to move around the auditorium talking to parents. My earlier vision seemed to be coming true of the mob. It was just a matter of time until the pitchforks came out. The prophecy was coming to pass. This was the beginning of the end.

I finished helping our guest speaker pack up and chatted with a few of the parents that hung around. Then I noticed that a small group of people had formed around this mom and some of those in the group were my key adult leaders. I walked towards them and got the attention of one, asking if she had a moment to talk about our upcoming mission trip—basically making things up to pull this group apart. Still, I wanted to stay close enough to hear what this mom was saying, so we did.

The youth leader I'd pulled away said, "Thank you, I didn't know how to get out of that!"

I took her tone as a bad sign. I trusted her as one of my key leaders, and I respected her opinion. It was then that I knew I was in trouble. I was pretty certain that there were people on the way to burn down my house. I started getting the attention of my other leaders and asking for their "help" with our "mission trip." At one point the mom and I caught each other's eyes, and I'm sure she was throwing daggers (pitchforks?) at me. The night finally finished and everyone went home. My house was not on fire, thank God, and there were no pitchforks in sight.

The mom and I were supposed to debrief afterwards on Monday. So naturally I called her on Thursday. We chatted about the night and her meeting. I apologized about the mix up with the room and assured her that it was booked. We talked through everything and nothing else came of it. I was saved.

As I look back I realize that I was afraid, and I allowed this fear to grow. You probably read the whole story thinking, "I don't get it… where is this fear coming from?" But that's the point! There was an evil lie whispered in my ear and I believed it. I let it taint the way I looked at the whole situation. I didn't shepherd this mom along as she was looking for prayer, support, and ideas for her own parenting. How could I? I was too busy assuring myself that she was the enemy and was out to get me! I didn't take time to listen to her heart, and more importantly I didn't listen to God through this whole situation. I allowed fear to control my thoughts and actions rather than truth.

STORY 28: CHAOS THEORY
by Ron Belsterling

Never underestimate the importance of two critical things to parents: organization and communication.

The youth group was going away for a weekend retreat. We had a great speaker lined up. We had a great place at the shore lined up. We had plenty of teens who wanted to go. We had parents who were both curious and encouraging. Everything was *great*. I was feeling like an organizational animal!

Except of course that my organization for the trip resembled a Picasso painting. Most of the pieces were there, but nothing really seemed to make sense.

I told the youth to get permission slips signed. But I didn't communicate much beyond that to the parents. And even then, many parents were quite unsure as to when the retreat was, where it was, how long it was, or how much it was costing. Oops. I remember the anxiety I was feeling on the morning of departure like it was yesterday. It was ugly.

I had no idea who really was going on the trip. I had never given anyone a deadline for making a deposit, turning in a permission slip, committing to going, etc. It seems the only piece of information that everyone understood was the date and time we were leaving for the retreat. Some youth who I expected to come showed up. Others I expected did not. Meanwhile some teens I knew nothing of were also joining us.

Parents were there with travel bags and questions. (I guess trusting the teens to share the key details with their parents was the wrong approach for effective communication.)

Who was chaperoning? (I was, that was a stupid question.) *How much was the trip and was there any type of "sliding scale" for teens who didn't have enough money?* (Umm… wasn't sure what that meant at the time. I only knew that if they were going they had to pay.) *Who was driving?* (Again, stupid question. I was.) *But didn't we have more young people than would fit in our broken down nine-passenger van?* (Oh, let's see now… hmm… Can any of you [present and presently angry parents] drive?) *Can I sign the permission slip for Johnny, my son's friend, because his parents aren't available right now?* (Sure. [But would that really count in an emergency???]) And there were many others…

Needless to say, we left several hours late. The retreat turned out to be great, *despite* its dreadful beginning. The enthusiasm it generated with the youth was momentous. But it also generated a large amount of frustration and apprehension with the parents. Looking back on that experience, I'm amazed that any of them let their children go with me that day. Yes, I was cool. But that didn't seem to matter to parents. Indeed, I was truly an "Organizing Animal!" Literally. That trip was organized about as well as if a chimp had done it. I had some work ahead of me to earn the trust of the parents.

Many of us who go into youth ministry are "people" people—we're not interested in details. We're often more heart-oriented than head-oriented. But details are important. Communication is important. And I never had that disastrous of a beginning to a trip again. I learned my lesson.

I learned to enlist the help of people who are good with organization. My wife is great with organization. I started running many plans by her to see what questions people would have that I took for granted. Additionally, I started using parents to help arrange some of the needed communication steps for me. Again, I would get the questions long *before* the trip was to occur. I started utilizing phone trees, and bulletins, and bulletin boards (which in modern times I guess would be group texts, web pages, and social media). I made deadlines for deposits and commitments. I eliminated exceptions (almost always). I created permission slips with two parts—one part with key information for parents to keep, and the other part for me. (For big trips I even required notarized slips.)

It was a long road but eventually I did get to the place where parents felt I was a good communicator and well organized. Having their trust is an invaluable asset and was well worth all the work. I just wish I hadn't started by digging myself into such a deep hole.

STORY 29: KNOW WHO YOU KNOW
by Ron Belsterling

"Ron, I really like you. But I still I find it really hard to forgive you."

These words were said to me out of the blue by one of my wife's good friends. She was very active in our church. She was a trooper. Great worker. Great attitude. Supportive, etc. She and my wife were incredible close. True friends.

I was shocked... what had I done?

It turns out, my crime took place years earlier, when I first started at the church. I had flippantly said some things at a meeting about a middle school Sunday school teacher's incompetence.

As I lived in a parsonage right beside the church, the middle school met in my basement during the Sunday school hour. This teacher was great relationally, but allowed the young people more latitude than I deemed appropriate. Most of the basement was quite a mess every Sunday when my family returned home. One night at the Christian Education (CE) meeting, I spared no insult of the teacher when imploring the CE Committee to approve the notion of moving the class out of my house.

No, my wife's friend was not the teacher in question—it was her husband. And she was serving on the CE committee at the time of my rant. I can't imagine how embarrassed she must have been. I'm the one who should have been embarrassed. Being that I had only started at the church month or two earlier, I knew first names of folks but not last names. Their children were not yet in the youth program. I'm sure everyone on the committee was shocked by my callous candor. No one said anything to me. Without much discussion, they approved and decided to advance my recommendation. In retrospect, I don't know if they actually supported the idea as much as they just wanted me to stop talking.

This woman was humiliated by me in front of others. Yet she and the others on the CE committee were unbelievably gracious in receiving the criticisms and not defensively chastising me or complaining about me to the church's leadership. Perhaps she was in shock. But how many other people would have passed up the chance to file a complaint? (And a totally legitimate one at that!)

Sometimes those of us in youth ministry complain to each other about how God's people are so critical and whiny. We often have no idea that there are some (and possibly many) who showed us extra doses of mercy and grace. James 3:6 says, "And the tongue is a fire" (ESV).

I was too quick to criticize, unmercifully, someone who actually was trying to do a job no one else wanted and one in which he was not gifted. Yet he was joyfully willing. He needed my assistance and gratitude, not my criticism. His wife needed my apology—and apologize I did. And did again. By the grace of God, I was maturing from year to year. By the grace of God, people like Mary allowed me the time to get to where I needed to be. By God's grace, I was fortunate to have a mature Christian in my congregation who had patience with me and forgave me. Her husband did too.

We need to know our people. We need to care about them enough to find out as quickly as possible who they are. We need to express gratitude to God for his people who work both for us and with us, and who have shown us his light. One of my constant prayers is to appreciate, not criticize. I encourage you to start praying the same.

STORY 30: THE GIFT OF RUDENESS
by Mark Oestreicher

During a critical time in my development as a leader, I was poorly mentored by two older pastors in the church I worked in at the time. They saw the non-existence of mercy in my spiritual gift mix (it was easy to spot, and they were the same way), and told me that my lack of mercy was actually a key component in the *strength* of my leadership (really, they actually said that). Almost sadder than their ridiculous input was the fact that I believed them—for a few years.

This wrong-headed assumption came crashing down in one day, while working in a different church: I made three different women cry in three subsequent meetings. When the first started crying, I thought to myself, "Well, that's what happens sometimes when you speak the truth. People don't want to face the truth." When the second woman started crying, I felt disoriented. Something was wrong, but I couldn't put my finger on it. But when the third woman started crying, I felt the brick-like thump of God's conviction upside my head.

So here's the misconception, as obvious as it might be: My natural lack of any particular spiritual gift is not permission to act the opposite! I might score in the negative numbers for mercy on spiritual gifts tests, but I am still called to live as a merciful person.

My experience with this misconception, in this particular area, may be extreme. But I see youth workers buying into this thinking all the time in more subtle ways. "I'm not creative." "I don't have the gifts or training to teach, or to lead a small group." Whatever.

Never use your lack of obvious gifting in an area as an excuse. When we do that, we rob ourselves of the opportunity to see God clearly work in and through us—and that's the stuff of the full living that Jesus talks about.

STORY 31: SPAGHETTI DINNER DISASTER
by Amy Jacober

The church was supportive and expected good things for the annual all-church dinner fundraiser. I was new to the church and it was my first time on staff, but this wasn't my first rodeo. As an experienced volunteer, a newly minted seminary graduate, and veteran of numerous summer camps, I thought, "How hard can hosting an evening be?"

By tradition, it was a dress-up evening with a meal served by the youth group, with the evening's entertainment provided in-house with an all-church talent show. I knew better than to take it all on by myself, but Sheila, the old saint, was known for putting together the talent show. Half the night was already covered. In fact, after years of doing this, she had an army of people joining her to pull off the show.

My inner overachiever kicked in, claiming I could do my part not only better than expected, but better than had ever been done before. I also mentally committed to making it look effortless—in order to give the glory to God, of course. I gathered my own little army of helpers: the youth made table decorations, our administrator went shopping, a parent created the program, and other parents prepared to wait tables and clean up afterwards. My team reflected the body of Christ, each doing their part.

The day came, and I arrived at church—a whole hour early—

determined to sail smoothly through the event. I was a planner extraordinaire. I was "Super Youth Pastor." Hands on hips and shimmering smile. Or at least that's what I thought at the time. Feeling confident, I knew it was time to begin cooking the spaghetti. I put the water on to boil, then set the tables and folded programs.

I learned the hard way that a watched pot never boils.

Two watched pots, really—each pot holding five gallons of water, truly never seemed to boil.

I never dreamed that the meal I made alone at home in twenty minutes would take *hours* when cooking for 200. My so-called early arrival was several hours too late. I thought I had enlisted all the help I needed. I even declined offers from our kitchen crew in the weeks leading up to the event. My motives were good. I wanted for them to have a break. In my enthusiasm, I never heard the advice they were trying to give and dismissed any overtures of guidance along the way.

I was so consumed with orchestrating every detail, I neglected to allow others to participate. I neglected to seek input or to learn from others. It wasn't that I was trying to do this alone. In fact, I was quite proud that I had listened and was working from my training to assemble a team. My problem wasn't a lack of people. It was a lack of experience and knowing what people I needed and what to do with the ones I had.

What should have been a meal and then a show, turned into groups of people eating very *al dente* pasta in shifts. The last plate was served to very hungry people just before the talent show ended. No one complained… to me, at least. In fact, several people came to my aid throughout the evening. I grew more and more frantic, more and more apologetic, and began making bad decisions to make up for a train wreck of a meal. We had to move tables, spilled sauce on the sanctuary carpet, and served less-than-edible meals hours late. It was clear by night's end that my "Super Youth Leader" card might be revoked.

The next day in the staff meeting, I was asked how I thought the night went. I was horrified and just glad it was over. I knew I had lost my cool the night before and wondered how they would ever trust me to take anyone to camp or possibly be in any stressful situation if I couldn't even handle spaghetti. I expected to be told I was on probation or my job was on the line. Instead, as I told of my embarrassment and failure, the staff nodded slowly and said, "We saw it coming."

What?

They saw the trainwreck coming and let it happen. They talked to me about lessons that can only be learned through experience, not words. They had seen young ministers so protected by leaders that they never made any mistakes on their own until it was too big, too damaging to be forgiven. They wanted me to fail in a church that had abundant grace so that I could learn how to get up again. They wanted me to experience the frustration I felt so poignantly that night so that the lessons would stick. I learned my lesson. There's no way I could forget it. The church staff exhibited grace by allowing a yearly tradition to become memorable for all the wrong reasons. They let me fail in a safe environment so I could learn how to get back up on my own when it counted.

Grace is a funny concept. I had taught on it and discussed it many times in youth ministry. I had even extended grace to others on numerous occasions as I sought to be an imitator of Christ as a leader and minister. What I didn't realize was how little I understood grace. It would have been easier for me had I been yelled at, punished somehow. I learned that was really my view of God; anger and wrath preceded grace in the atonement I knew. What I experienced however was unadulterated grace. A different atonement. No probation, no false pretense or bait and switch. They knew what I had done wrong, confronted me openly about it, and extended grace. It was humbling in ways that are still profound to me today.

SECTION III: REFLECTIONS

 Jen Bradbury @ymjen　　　　　　　September 28
My game #fail involved mayo, ice cream, & very
unhappy parents...

It is sometimes the case that we youth workers see parents in a
less than positive light. They don't get what we are doing. They are
sometimes seen as a problem, and a problem that needs to be solved,
at that. This is especially true for younger youth workers. We both
remember thinking, when we were 20 or so, of how awful it would be
to be 40. Who would even want to even be alive when they were *that*
old?

Happily, though, as we age, we tend to begin to see parents as
potential partners. We realize we are not the parents of these
teenagers. We remember, they are the parents, we are not. The
sociologists who study these things again and again affirm that it is
parents who have, by far, the most influence with young people when
it comes to all aspects of life, including faith.

Several of the stories in this section show that lack of communication
(youth worker to parent) was a large component of the toxicity
experienced by all. We gather, then, that being more intentional
about communicating plans is important. The nice thing about
communication, if we are good at it, is that it conveys our care and
responsibility, even if parents don't read our emails, tweets, texts,
or other social media postings or yet-to-be-invented means of
communication.

As for volunteers, we have both realized in our own ministries that
no one person has all the gifts, strengths, and personality styles that
are out there... but as a team, we do. This epiphany sometimes comes
with a bit of sorrow mixed in. When our group has grown to the
point where we know we can't do it all by ourselves, something both
wonderful and threatening can happen. Some of our youth will share

their deepest hurts and joys *not* with us, but with someone else on the team. If we see that as wonderful (though perhaps painful) we are well on our way to a mature understanding of leadership.

From Jonathan...
I completely shifted my approach to volunteers based on a friend's critique. I now plan my leader's meeting to focus primarily on encouragement and celebration. What about training? Sure, it's there. But now there's a desire for it. Now there's a hunger. I do my best to empower them as leaders, and not just by buying a book on youth ministry and putting it in their hands. We talk a lot about pastoring youth but it is also our job to pastor our leaders, making sure they are in a healthy place and ministering out of the overflow.

We noticed, and learned it the hard way, that things go better with parents *and* volunteers when the ministry has a clear mission/vision/core values statement. It helps people see what the big picture goal of the ministry is. (Need an example? Just Google "youth ministry core values.")

Questions for Reflection and Discussion

1. Think of an issue you have had with a parent. In what way would better communication have helped?

2. Your parents or guardians ... you had one or two, to be sure. In what way has your relationship or lack of relationship with your own parents impacted—positively or negatively—your attitude about and relationship with the parents/guardians of the youth in your ministry?

3. If you are leading volunteers, which of these are you the best at: *enfolding* (recruiting them and helping them feel part of a team), *encouraging* (affirming their successes and being missional yourself about giving them positive feedback), *equipping* (providing practical "how to" training for their role as

a volunteer), and *unleashing* (providing ministry responsibilities that are in sync with their own strengths, personality, gifts, and passions)?

4. In which of these four, mentioned in question three, might you need some improvement? How will you improve?

Major Project Ideas for the Classroom

1. Write an eight-page paper or prepare a 45-minute seminar that discusses the similarities between coaching a sports team and leading a staff of volunteers in youth ministry. Cite at least five books as resources as well as five websites.

2. Search online for "managing volunteers best practices." Also search on Amazon with those words. Write an eight-page paper on the most applicable insights you gleaned from the resources, or prepare a 60-minute seminar for youth workers on this topic.

3. Find three books for Christian parents that have excellent reviews and read them. Interview ten parents of teenagers. Questions should include:
    *   *What is the most enjoyable part of raising teenagers?*
    *   *What are some of the stress points for you of raising teenagers?* (You may have the opportunity to recommend one of the books you've read.)
    *   *How can a youth pastor be a better support and encouragement to you as a parent?*

Write up your results. Interview five youth pastors who feel they are doing well when it comes to parents. Write up your results. Work both your write-ups into a 45-minute seminar for youth workers.

"A man can fail many times, but he isn't a failure until he begins to blame somebody else."

John Burroughs

"My great concern is not whether you have failed, but whether you are content with your failure."

Abraham Lincoln

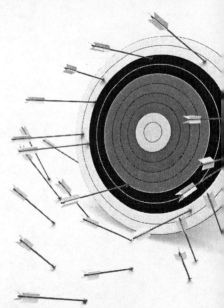

SECTION IV: FAILURES WITH CHURCH LEADERSHIP

mistakes made with senior pastors
or other leadership in the church or organization

SECTION IV: INTRODUCTION

> "Do not fear mistakes. You will know failure. Continue to reach out."
>
> Benjamin Franklin

We have both learned—sometimes the hard way—that youth ministry is not only about having the fundamentals right, it's not only about working with youth, it's not only about learning how to enfold/encourage/equip/unleash volunteers and parents. Youth ministry is about being on good terms with "those above"—our senior pastors, church elders, ministry board, or others "higher up" the leadership structure in our churches or ministry organizations.

The poignant stories in this section represent a good cross-section of issues. While all the issues addressed are important, we believe most important is one's attitude about and relationship with the senior pastor or ministry director (Stories 33 and 34.)

A business book from the '90s titled *Orbiting the Giant Hairball: A Corporate Fool's Guide to Surviving with Grace*[12] urges employees not to let organizational structures, procedures, rules, and less-than-perfect leaders dissuade us from the pursuit of excellence. We agree that sometimes even in the church or parachurch organization things can get complicated, but we affirm the importance of nevertheless enjoying the journey in a spirit of thanksgiving. Without those above us, very likely our ministry in a particular place wouldn't even exist.

---

12. MacKenzie, Gordon. *Orbiting the Giant Hairball: A Corporate Fool's Guide to Surviving with Grace* (New York: Viking Press, 1996).

STORY 32: SURE, I CAN PAINT THAT FELLOWSHIP HALL
by Les Christie

I had just arrived as a part-time youth worker in a Garden Grove, California, church. I noticed the walls of the youth room were a dingy, hospital-white color, so I suggested to the youth that we paint the room. I rounded up cans of donated paint and met with the teens at 7:00 a.m. the next Saturday. They couldn't agree on a single color, so we compromised by using a different can on each wall. We painted one wall white, one wall black, and the last two red and blue. We cleaned up and went out to breakfast. Mission accomplished.

What I did not know was that another group met in that room. During the first service, when the youth were in church, the senior citizens had a class there.

I remember sitting on the stage in the service. I was beaming with pride and joy. The youth had done great work, and I felt excited about being in ministry. Then the senior pastor slid into the chair next to me and told me how upset the senior citizens were. He told me I could kiss my job goodbye, and that he couldn't save me—that I was dead meat.

I immediately slipped out of the service and went into the senior citizens' class. Before they could say anything, I asked if they had noticed the room had been painted. They had. I then told them how excited I was to work in a church were the high school students were so spiritual.

I explained that the wall on the left was blue to symbolize heaven. The wall on the right was red to symbolize the blood of Christ. The wall behind them was black, which stood for sin, and they were facing away from that wall. The wall at the front of the room was white, which stood for purity. What could they say?

I then grabbed the teens and told them if anyone should ever ask them why we selected these colors, that's what they should say.

Epilogue: *Those colors remained in that room for the next 15 years. No one could paint over the blood of Jesus.*

STORY 33: GOLFING WITH THE SENIOR PASTOR
by Ron Belsterling

Early in my youth ministry career, while at one church, the senior pastor and I went golfing semi-regularly. It's just that he didn't know it.

To say that my senior pastor and I didn't get along would be a drastic understatement. He resented my presence seemingly from day one. No matter what I did, it was wrong. (I'm sure no other youth pastor can relate to this—*sarcasm*). If I was in the church on an afternoon, I should have been out contacting young people. If I was out, he told me I should have been in my office to be available to parents. If the staff was having lunch together, he joked to the others, "We can't swear today, Ron's with us." As if my dislike for foul language was a childish problem. He couldn't understand my resistance to having a youth outreach event with kegs of beer. (This is 100% true. The last youth pastor had over 100 teens hanging out in the parking lot—the kegs were in the bushes!) Though I have a carefree personality, I started getting migraine headaches on the mornings of staff meetings.

In our church we usually had a bunch of leftover bulletins every week. These included a small picture of the face of the senior pastor. So as not to waste good paper and printing, I decided to make use of them. I cut out the pictures and taped them to old golf balls—only for the purpose of uniquely identifying them of course. And, since I was a bad golfer—frequently sending many balls into the woods or into the

144

pond—I found that I was no longer bothered when these "poor" shots occurred. In fact, my game both improved and got worse. I started becoming more precise with my aim, but my scores climbed.

The worst part of this behavior is that I went golfing with guys from the youth group. I'm embarrassed to admit this. Many teenagers struggle with resistance to authority as it is. The last thing they need is an immature youth pastor modeling passive-aggressive disrespect for authority, let alone their church's senior pastor. I lament doing that with those young men to this day. I demonstrated such an immature way of communicating and dealing with my frustrations. Additionally, these balls could easily have been found by others in the community, potentially leading to who-knows-what for our church, the pastor, myself, etc. Hitting a pillow in private would have been smarter.

> ## DON'T DO THIS
>
> "I was once $20,000 over budget. It was a wealthy church and I had a good-sized budget (about $40,000). But, wow... $20,000 over budget. To this day I can't tell you how I wasn't fired. They did, however, assign a board member to "mentor" me in my spending practices from that point onward."
>
> Jonathan Hobbs

Worse yet, this was just a sign of what I was really doing—suppressing my feelings instead of working through them. Burying my frustrations was interfering in my ministry competence and even my marriage relationship, as I started having more arguments with my wife (my fault). It says in 1 Peter 2:12-13, "Always let others see you behaving properly... The Lord wants you to obey all human authorities, especially the Emperor" (CEV). This verse, and a book by David Augsburger, in which he used the phrase "care-frontation," convicted me.[13] (The book has been recently republished, and I highly recommend it.) I learned to trust the Lord and to say what needed to be said, always with respect, to the appropriate person or people. No matter the consequences. I always believed that truth prevails, but I needed to start living into that.

---

13. Augsburger, David. *Caring Enough to Confront: How to Understand and Express Your Deepest Feelings Toward Others* (Grand Rapids: Revell: [1973 as *The Love Fight*] 2009).

From that point forward, with respect and the motive to improve ministry and relationships, I had honest relationships with elders and pastors. I sought ways to follow the principles in Matthew 18 in the right spirit (i.e., with lots of prayer). That helped me to have more wholesome and appropriate relationships with my authorities

and with those under my spiritual authority—and with my family. Moving ahead in prayer and on principle (not pride), has been something that God has blessed—and he always will.

STORY 34: TALKING BEHIND THE SENIOR PASTOR'S BACK

by Ryan Sidhom

In the movie *The Devil's Advocate*, Al Pacino (playing the part of the Prince of Darkness) says, "Vanity. Definitely my favorite sin."[14] When I quote this, I tend to get it wrong. I always want to substitute "pride" in place of "vanity." Or maybe subconsciously I just think "pride" is more accurate…

Like many of my colleagues, I entered the world of youth ministry with a lot of passion. I was so on fire that I accepted a full-time position at a small church offering part-time pay. So, with a Bible in one hand and a water gun in the other—with which to extinguish the fiery darts of the enemy—I jumped into the crazy world of professional ministry.

I estimate I was putting in 50-60 hours a week. And even though I was working way more than I should have been—and paid even less—I loved every second! I loved planning programs and events, putting discipleship strategies into place, and preaching the Word of God.

Not surprisingly, the church members and staff affirmed my work and my passion. No one seemed to ask if I was taking enough personal time. They were so impressed, they changed my title from youth pastor

---

14. *The Devil's Advocate*, dir. by Taylor Hackford (Warner, 1997).

to associate pastor, which came with more responsibility but also a raise. The senior pastor also offered to expand my responsibilities by allowing me to cast vision to the entire congregation, as well as lead and direct vision ministry teams with the intent of moving an older and somewhat irrelevant church and congregation into a place where we were able to effectively reach members of the younger generation.

Of course, with this responsibility came a lot of pride. Here I was, a young man who had been in ministry for only a few short years. I had no seminary education. And I felt like I was being handed the keys!

I saw that the congregation was really getting behind my ideas, the Spirit seemed to be moving, and it was contagious. To add to the excitement, the congregation started to grow at rates unknown to that church in over five decades.[15] The excitement even started going beyond our walls and into the community. Other pastors in the city were excited for us and started asking for the "secret" to our church growth.

I think Al Pacino got it wrong. I'm pretty sure pride is the devil's favorite sin…

As you may have suspected, the pride began to turn to arrogance. I became known as a "know-it-all" of sorts, and the terrible thing is I gladly accepted the label. I started to have a permanent posture of "I told you so." The pride monster grew, and I should have relocated my office to the ivory tower.

The senior pastor and I started to have some major disagreements on everything from service flow to finances to whether the toilet paper should be fed over the roll or under the roll.[16] The growing tension got to the point where we wouldn't even talk to each other aside from

---

15. Minor disclaimer: In the interest of not wanting to mislead you, the reader, I should note that while the growth in attendance was wonderful, we in no way ever came close to being a mega-church. Far from it. Even at the peak of our growth, most people reading this would have considered us a "small" church. The staff didn't grow to be more than the custodian, the secretary, children's director, myself, and the senior pastor.

16. The correct answer is OVER.

staff meetings, which was pretty sad since he and I were the only people on the pastoral staff.

The disagreements became more and more ridiculous. The disdain grew from a professional one into something much more personal. I went from disagreeing with him to being unable to stand being around him. I grew bitter and started avoiding him altogether. It got to the point where any time we were in the same room, there were arguments.

So where did it end? Did I lead a revolt? Did the church split? Did I have a major moral failure and end up on the front page of every newspaper in the city? No. In fact, all that happened was a conversation.

As the tempers were rising on a daily basis, I was approached after an evening meeting by a member of the congregation who also happened to have a disinclination towards the senior pastor. He started complaining about the senior pastor, and I should have defended the authority that God had placed over me. Instead, I not only agreed with the disgruntled parishioner, but I *added my own list* to his catalog of grievances. I went on and on, and it's so scary how that conversation felt *great* at the time. There was so much energy— and it felt just like the vision-casting I had been doing. "Wouldn't it be great if…" And if nothing else, it was so good to finally get all that stuff off my chest. I remember leaving the church that night with a sense of *accomplishment*.

The next morning, the whole conversation from the night before hit me like a ton of bricks. I began to weep uncontrollably. The conviction that came over me was nothing short of overwhelming. Everything about the last few years was coming up, and all I could see was how blind I had been. I was the prodigal associate pastor wanting my inheritance and wishing my overseer was gone, so I could have it all. I was a naive spoiled brat, whining and complaining when I didn't get my way.

I called the man with whom I'd had the conversation. He assured me that he wouldn't tell anyone what I said, and that he forgave me. I felt like the gorilla on my back jumped off, and all that remained was the elephant that it was riding on.

The next day came, and I went to the church, walked right into the senior pastor's office, and closed the door behind me. I sat down and told him everything. I told him about the bitterness I'd been harboring in my heart. I told him about the arrogance that was so prevalent in my life. I told him that I understood God had placed him in the position of leadership for a reason, and that I was completely at fault for questioning his authority. I told him that I had talked about him behind his back, and that I had spoken to the individual, apologized, and that I would never do it again. And then I asked for him to forgive me.

He looked at me, pursed his lips, and said "No. No, I don't forgive you. What you did was wrong, and I don't think I can forgive you for it."

I was more than just a little shocked. That's not what's supposed to happen... right? I acted on my conviction. I had prayed—hard! I'd confessed. I was humbled. I had come down from the tower and laid it all out on the table. I was supposed to be forgiven and we'd move forward and be a stronger team, and God was going to use us in huge ways!

But that's not how it went down. He said, "No."

What came next was a whirlwind of pain and confusion. Not long after my confession, it was decided by both parties (myself and the personnel committee) that I should step down from my position at the church.

I don't fault the pastor for his decision not to forgive me. Our relationship had gotten poisonous, and it wasn't healthy for the church. Something had to change, and I guess he felt that I needed to move on. I also have no doubt that my actions were hurtful to him. I'd slowly been undercutting him for years. The conversation was just the more obvious of the strikes.

I've learned that respecting the authority over you is a major aspect of healthy ministry. I know too many youth directors who feel like God is calling them to go against "the powers that be." They see themselves as David the shepherd boy, and the elders—or deacons or senior pastors—as Goliath, forgetting that they're meant to be a team.

The perfect boss doesn't exist. The only perfect boss we have is the Jewish carpenter we all work for. After that, we're all just a bunch of sinners who share office space.

STORY 35: CONTRACT NEGOTIATIONS
by Alisa Laska

When I first applied for my current ministry position, it was listed as 30 hours a week. However, as I began talking with the search committee, it appeared that something else was on the table. The church, it turned out, owned a house that was currently sitting vacant. They explained that they were considering offering housing in exchange for an additional ten hours per week, which would be spent working with the preteens of the church, a growing population at the time.

With some reservations about working with a broad age range, I did agree, and we renegotiated. The committee went to the church board, and the house was offered as a part of my salary. It all sounded great, especially since my husband and I were newly married and would be moving to a new area that was incredibly expensive to live in. We were very happy to have a single-family house to call home, not just a tiny condo an hour away. This house was right next to the church!

The HR committee set up a contract with us for the house, listing things like who would pay the trash and electric bills, who would mow the lawn, and what would happen if something needed to be fixed. We also set up a system where the whole thing would be reviewed every couple of years to see if it was still working for us and for the church.

It actually ended up working out pretty well for a while. We lived in the house for five years, and it helped us to be able to save up money to buy our own home in such a high-priced housing market. Of course, it wasn't perfect. We'd occasionally have someone stop by to get a church key because they'd been locked out. We also had various things go wrong with the house, such as the time that the sewage system backed up into our basement. For those who've lived on church property, I feel your pain. (As I was mopping up stinky water, I found myself questioning the whole thing.) Overall, however, it was a good situation.

The problem came when we were ready to move out and buy our own home. I was about to give birth to my first child and of course everyone recognized that we'd want a bigger house with more space that we could call our own. They were fine with us moving out, and we gave them plenty of notice. The tough part came when I mentioned my salary. I had been hired five years prior, so there were different board members and new staff members in place. The people who had been involved in my hiring were no longer in leadership—and some had even moved away.

DON'T DO THIS

"Back when smartphones and apps were still very new, I spent hundreds of dollars of the church's money on a few games. It almost became something of an addiction. Because the technology was still very new, the powers-that-be never figured out what I was doing. I've never told them, but I continued giving to the church long after I left as a way of trying to make up for what I did."

Name Withheld

As I talked with our senior pastor about the situation, he made it clear that he believed the house was a perk of my job and not part of my salary. He expected that I would still work full-time hours when I moved out. To me, this was not what I understood at my hiring. Although he had not been involved in my hiring process, he felt he was doing what was in the best interest of the church. I felt that God had put me under his authority and I shouldn't question it, but I knew with absolute certainty that the house was not a perk but was a part of my salary. This, along with other issues along the way, didn't feel like how the church should be the church.

And it's at this point in the story where I really want to go on a rant about the things I feel that other people did wrong in this situation. However, I'm not here to focus on the hurt I felt, but the mistakes I made along the way. I know the pastor wasn't trying to be unreasonable and the committee members didn't want me to be hurt, but through the process I was left with some scars.

After that conversation with my pastor, I put in a proposal to our HR committee. I spent hours drawing up the proposal, as well as copying supporting documents from when I was hired and the original ad for my job that listed 30 hours on it. I proposed that when I moved out of the house they could either pay me for the additional ten hours a week if they were able, or I could change my workload to 30 hours a week. I met with appropriate people from the church, including the head of HR, gave them the packet, and went over everything. And then I waited. And waited.

Three months later when I got the news, I was out on maternity leave and was exhausted mentally and physically from being drooled on and having to change hundreds of diapers. I received a bombshell of a letter from the HR committee stating that they had denied my request. I could move out of the house, but I would not receive any additional compensation. And I would continue to work 40 hours a week.

It was a horrible time to receive bad news. I was really broken up about it. I knew what they decided was wrong. I was frustrated, but I knew I had to rest under the church and pastor's authority. I prayed and prayed about it and also about my attitude. I knew it wasn't fair for them to ask me to work ten hours a week for free, but it looked like that was how it would have to be.

A month or two later, I ended up talking to a good friend of mine who has also been in youth ministry for a long time. He encouraged me not to give up. While talking to him, we thought of the idea of talking to my church's treasurer. We knew that she had been around for a long time and knew about my hiring process. She wrote my paychecks and knew that the house was part of my salary, because we were in fact taxed on it. I asked her if she would explain this to the HR committee, and she did.

This ended up as a year-long process of negotiation. The HR committee finally agreed that when we moved out, I would be able to lower my hours to 30, and I was overjoyed. Finally, they understood where I was coming from. My pastor asked me to delegate much of my workload to volunteers, and I agreed simply for the fact that I just wanted to get on with the ministry.

Now it's been a few years since this happened, and I can see God's hand in it as I look at what I've learned and where it has gotten my family and my ministry. I really love our church and working here has been a joy and a privilege. We have wonderful youth leaders and great teens. The church is welcoming and caring and threw me a huge baby shower when I was pregnant. Looking back, this incredibly emotional negotiation issue could have been avoided if I'd thought it through and gotten every detail in writing ahead of my hiring.

STORY 36: SALARY SURPRISE
by Jonathan Hobbs

The next year's budget was passed around for review and approval at a church board meeting. I had been working part-time at the church for three years, and I'd had conversations with the leadership about how I needed to go full time in the coming year or I wouldn't be able to stay in seminary and would have to move on to another job. As I turned to the part of the budget that included staff salaries, I saw that my salary was staying at part time. I started to cry. I held it back as best as I could, but as we discussed the budget, I spoke… started sobbing, and said, "I guess this means I have to turn in my resignation." (Actually, I kind of shouted it.)

Yes, it would have been nice for someone to have met with me before the meeting and let me know about this, but it was a major failure on my part to get overly emotional in the moment. It really wasn't the end of the world.

It is, however, what led to me moving on to a full-time position a few months later. And looking back, if I'd wanted to stay there another year or two I probably could have figured out something. The rest of the board did not know of my conversations with the pastor and treasurer, so I could have simply brought it up.

I was thinking far too small. My actions didn't *start* a conversation— which is what was needed in that moment. All I saw was my world collapsing… and as it collapsed I started grasping for… well, anything. The result was a sobbing, dramatic mess of a moment that left a lot of people confused and didn't leave a lot of room for healing.

I was also incredibly tunnel-visioned. I couldn't tell you another thing about that budget. Other stuff had been cut and other requests had been denied. But I was really only worried about me.

STORY 37: SAME PAGE?
by Les Christie

My first paid position in youth ministry came at the age of 19. I was attending college and found a part-time position at a church in Compton, California. This was in the late 1960s. It was just after the infamous Watts riots.[17] Racial tensions were high. The church I worked in seemed, at first appearance, to have been successful at peaceful community relationships, despite being mostly white. The youth group I worked with had teens from several ethnic backgrounds and we began to grow. We went from about six teens to 30 in a few months.

That was when the senior pastor asked for my resignation. I never knew why. He had only been there a few months himself. He informed me that the elders had come to this decision. I was somewhat surprised since most of the elders had kids in the youth group, and they seem so pleased with what was happening with their kids and the ministry.

Thirty years later I got a telephone call from this same pastor. He

---

17. Quick History Lesson: On August 11, 1965, an African-American driver was arrested for drunk-driving in the Watts neighborhood of Los Angeles. A minor roadside argument escalated into a riot that lasted for six days. There was looting and arson, especially of white-owned businesses. About 4,000 members of the California National Guard were called in to assist. Thirty-four deaths, $40 million in damage. It was the city's worst unrest until the Rodney King riots of 1992.

called because his son had attended one of my seminars where I had mentioned that I'd worked in Compton. He asked his dad if he knew me. His dad had long ago left the Compton church, but his son's question brought back some memories and unfinished business. He called me and explained that the reason why I had been let go. It seemed one of the older elders whose kids were grown had told the senior pastor that either I had to go or the senior pastor had to go, because I was reaching too many youth from different ethnic backgrounds for his liking. The young senior pastor decided I would have to leave. The pastor told me over the phone that less than one year after I left that racially bigoted elder's white daughter married a black man. The elder died three months later of what appeared to be a stress-related heart attack.

Looking back on it, I realize though I was excited about my first real job in youth ministry, I never really had any discussions with the church leadership about what their vision for the church was. I assumed they would be excited about a youth ministry that reached community youth. I was wrong. And I know what you're thinking— *but that elder's vision was awful!*

You're right. It was. But the more important lesson here is that I didn't *know* it. I was completely blindsided. Come to think of it, so was the senior pastor. I bet together we could have taken a stand… but to do that, it really helps for everyone to be on the same page first.

SECTION IV: REFLECTIONS

AngryYouthPastor @AngryYouthGuy   June 15
My senior pastor had his birthday today. I'm starting to wonder if leaving a wheelchair and an IV drip in his office was a bit much.

We understand now that youth ministry involves getting a lot of things right, at least much of the time. Here we've added being on good terms withour superiors to the list.

Though we are in total awe of Les Christie's (God inspired?) quick-thinking in front of the senior citizens whose room at the church he had creatively painted (Story 32), he did learn that in a church situation there are usually specific and proper channels through which changes like are to be made. The churches we are in now each have a committee or system for anything building related, whether it's regarding event locations or cosmetic changes. The people on the "property management" or buildings-and-grounds team are not our adversaries, but they need to be in the loop if we want to build, paint, or in any way alter something.

Similarly, we have learned not to view the budget/money people in the church as the enemy. We realize these people do not necessarily control how much money the church receives. We realize if the amount that comes in is below the budgeted amount, the finance team has to say no to things. It's not meant to be personal. The stories from Jonathan and Alisa, however, are very personal and very painful. It is really important for youth workers to understand the big picture of the church or parachurch budget and the concept of cash flow.[18] That's why those in charge of the budget often want to know in advance if we have big summer expenses. Giving is usually down in

---

18. As you probably know, that term is simply the concept of how much money comes in compared to how much goes out in a given month.

summer, so cash needed during summer needs to be put aside during the winter and spring.

From Len...
I learned the hard way why it is important to see the big picture of finances. I made an impassioned plea for a large budget increase for our growing youth ministry. The dreams were consistent with the church's vision, and I was certain the money people would see the legitimacy of my proposals. The treasurer pulled me aside after a meeting. We had a good relationship, he knew I was fanatical about turning in receipts and generally being a good steward. "So Len, I'm sorry, we need to turn down your request. Remember the church budget, when it comes to youth ministry, includes your salary and benefits, the salaries of your four (!!) interns, all the expenses for the two church vans and one church bus. The 4,000 square feet of new youth ministry space your ministry moved into last year cost the church $5,000 per month in interest payments on the mortgage. We feel the crucial needs of other church ministries need to be addressed, so for now please be content with what you have." What could I say to that?

Beyond money and facilities, however, we believe the most important stories in this chapter relate to one's relationship with and attitude toward the senior pastor. Ron (Story 33) and Ryan (Story 34) have been very open with us regarding their own sin here. It is easy to assume that all senior pastors or parachurch directors will exhibit the fruit of the Spirit (Galatians 5:22-23) and have been wonderfully trained to be affirming, affiliative, and empowerment-filled leaders under whose leadership we will always hear the angels singing. Always filled with the fruit of the Spirit? Always geared to encourage and empower us? Not likely.

From Len...
One pastor I served under developed a very distracting habit in the pulpit of exclaiming "Right?!" about every third sentence. For three

Sundays (God, please forgive me), I kept track how many times he said this is his 30-minute sermon. The average was 85 times per sermon. I met with him, expressed my genuine appreciation for his many positive qualities, and asked if it was okay if I made a suggestion which would make something very good (his preaching) even better. He, with a little hesitation, agreed. I told him what I came in to tell him. He sat in silence for a moment, and responded "That can't be right." We parted amicably but not warmly, and I affirmed my heart was only to make something good even better. A week later, he called me into his office. With a smile on his face, he said, "You were wrong last week, Len. I listened to the sermons and the average was 81 per sermon, not 85. Thanks, I had no idea." Whew!

From Jonathan...
When I have spoken about "respecting your leadership" to youth ministry college students, I'm always amazed about how much pushback I get. Maybe it's because I use the dreaded S-word: submission. (Horrors!) But I think it has a lot more to do with these young people walking into their first jobs with the wrong attitude–or maybe a better way to say it is that they've taken the wrong posture.

Years ago, during the Q&A time at a leadership event, I stood up and asked pastor and author Craig Groeschel, "How can I effectively lead up? How can I influence the people above me?" It was a gutsy thing to ask, given my boss was sitting right next to me! I don't have the space (or the copyrights) here to tell you everything Craig said in his answer, but his primary point was that of honoring those above us and making sure we take a posture of humility.[19]

Let me be blunt. At times, you will have better ideas, be funnier and more engaging, and have a clearer sense of where the church is headed than your senior pastor. This does not mean that you are allowed to disrespect the authority that God has placed over you. I've actually heard young youth directors use the same "David and Goliath"

19. A few years later I heard Craig do an entire talk about "leading up." I want him to know 1) thanks for finally answering the question, 2) I guess I inspired you to write a talk, so... you're welcome, and 3) if you need more ideas for talks, I have plenty more questions.

comparative reference that Ryan used in his story in this section. But we tend to forget that this is not a story of someone under another person's authority. However, the story of David and Saul is, and perhaps that's a story we should study a little more closely. We must learn well to "lead under" the leadership above us, and have a heart of care for them as well.

We both make it a practice to pray often for the head pastor, say only good things about the pastor in public, not assume we know better than he or she does (about anything, though we may suspect we do), and if we have an issue with the senior pastor, speak privately with him or her about it, sandwiched with ample affirmation of the gifts and good qualities that person posesses.

Questions for Reflection and Discussion

1. Talk about a boss you have had in the past who was considerably less than perfect. What about him or her did you find most frustrating?

2. In the church or other Christian ministry, have you ever had a poor relationship with someone above you—the pastor, another church leader like an elder, board member, or treasurer? If so, can you think of any way in which you contributed to that poor relationship?

3. How do you view the "red tape" that is so common in ministry? For example, do you have to "sign up" for rooms you use in the church? Describe any benefits you can think of from the procedures your church or organization have in place that you are expected to follow.

4. Think about the person just above you in your ministry. What are five good qualities about him or her for which you can be grateful? If your relationship with that "just above" person is excellent, are there any people in ministry you know who are suffering under difficult circumstances in this regard? What can

you do, even today, to encourage them?

Major Project Ideas for the Classroom

1. Search online using the phrase "youth pastor senior pastor relationship." Take a look at the first 15-20 of the 600,000-plus entries. Take special note of the commonalities. Take special note if any of the points or ideas in one resource are in direct opposition to those of another. Write a five-page paper including the following:
    *   Positives for the church when the senior pastor/youth pastor's relationship is excellent.
    *   Negatives for the church when the senior pastor/youth pastor's relationship is rocky.
    *   Develop a 30-minute workshop on this topic for senior pastors. Develop a 30-minute workshop on this topic for youth pastors.

2. Contact five senior pastors and interview them regarding their experiences (positive or negative) in having a youth pastor as part of their church staff. In all likelihood they'll have a lot to say. What one thing do they wish they would have known before their first experience of this?

3. Take a look at http://www.christianitytoday.com/le/leadership-training/. Scroll through the articles and find three that have to do with staff relations. Write a one-page reflection on each of the three.

"An essential aspect of creativity is not being afraid to fail."
Edwin Land

"Success is not built on success. It's built on failure. It's built on frustration. Sometimes it's built on catastrophe."
Sumner Redstone

SECTION V
FAILURES THAT DEFY CATEGORIZATION

mistakes in a class all their own

SECTION V: INTRODUCTION

> "Far better is it to dare mighty things, to win glorious triumphs, even though checkered by failure... than to rank with those poor spirits who neither enjoy nor suffer much, because they live in a gray twilight that knows not victory nor defeat."
>
> Theodore Roosevelt

Last but most certainly not least, here are stories we couldn't easily put in the other categories. Some of these mistakes are truly jaw-droppingly epic. Admittedly, this section is much "lighter" than many of the others. All the stories, save one, are told in a comedic tone and invite you to just laugh along with the author at the insanity of the situation. There is an underlying message with all of the stories here that simply says, "Did this really just happen?!" We find ourselves there a lot in ministry—for better or worse. And these are the stories of the "worse."

You'll hear about everything from painting projects to prostitution. You'll get great dating advice and learn how not to edit a movie. You'll double-check that you've booked the buses, and you'll think twice about booking the big name band. You might never again be able to look at baseball, beaches, and evangelism in the same way.

Above all we hope that you find yourself saying, "That seriously happened?" To which we say, "Sadly... yes. Yes, it did."

It might be nice for you to hear that not one of these authors lost a job, faced a lawsuit, or went to jail (at least not for the things in these stories). Since both of us have pieces in this section, we can personally testify to the fact that there is a God in heaven who does the miraculous... and we are exceedingly grateful!

STORY 38: RETREAT IN A HOUSE OF PROSTITUTION?
by Len Kageler

As far as I know, I am the only youth worker in all of Christendom to ever have a youth retreat in a house of prostitution.

Thinking back, the sign behind the registration desk did strike me as being odd: "No illegal activities allowed on the premises." But I shook it off and checked us in. Having confirmed that the motel had received our full payment a month earlier, I walked back out to help the senior high students unload the church bus. The retreat was going great. On Friday night we had slept on the floor of a church near Whistler Mountain, British Columbia (which hosted the Winter Olympics in 2010). On Saturday we skied Whistler and were excited about the rest of the weekend in the beautiful city of Vancouver, British Columbia. City Motel was now our headquarters.

A police car roared in from Main Street and stopped a yard from where I was standing. The officer got out and approached me. Looking like he was confused, or lost, or something, he asked me: "What are you doing?"

"Well, officer," I replied, "as you can see here, we're unloading the church bus. We skied Whistler today and will either ski Grouse Mountain tomorrow or chill out in Stanley Park. We're staying here tonight."

"Don't you know what this place is?"

My heart rate immediately skyrocketed. "What do you mean?"

"This is a house of prostitution… serves this end of the city." He turned his eyes away from me and looked around at the 45 or so teens and staff who were gathered closely around. "Better keep a close watch on your kids."

"Thanks…" my voice trailed off as he returned to the patrol car and speed off into the darkness.

My mind was a blur… we had no extra cash to find different lodging. I wasn't going to put lodging somewhere else on my credit card, because I knew the church was in financial-shortfall mode and it might be months before I would be reimbursed. And besides, we probably couldn't find another hotel for 50 people at that late hour. The entire group had heard my conversation with the police officer. No wonder City Motel was so cheap in the travel directory! Just wait until news of this one gets out: "Youth pastor jailed for his own protection as angry parents picket church."

Our bus driver that trip was Sam. He was also an elder in our church. He and I walked around to the other side of the bus so we could have a private conversation. We stood there speechless for about a minute before, finally, Sam whispered, "I think God wants to redeem this place tonight. I say we stay." I was feeling the same way.

I announced to the group, "We're gonna be fine," and we moved into our rooms.

But the rooms were so incredibly dirty—the towels were paper thin and stained—most of us came right back out to the bus to get the sleeping bags we used the night before when we camped out on the floor of the church. I gathered the whole group in my room (no small task given its modest size). We talked openly about our predicament. We talked about Sam's sense that God had a purpose for us here (of all places). With that, we pulled out the guitars and started a raucous worship service and prayer meeting. *It was glorious.*

Just as the officer predicted, it was a very busy night. Male and female customers came and went all night long. Most of us didn't sleep very well. We left City Motel Sunday morning (after more worship and prayer) and had a great day skiing and going around the city.

The ride home was three hours long, which gave me a lot of time to wonder what would happen upon our arrival. Sam was thinking about this too. In the church parking lot on our return, he spoke to as many parents as he could connect with and phoned the rest within the next day. He explained the situation, that their kids were safe the whole time, and that it wasn't wrong to have teens see a sinful, immoral environment and how sadly dreadful it was. None of their kids were ever without staff presence; and furthermore, it was a great opportunity to bring light into a very dark place. Thank God Sam had immense respect within the congregation for his discernment and spiritual depth. And—a miracle as far as I'm concerned—no parent ever complained or argued about the decision we made.

My suggestions to you based on this experience? First, don't book accommodations for youth group events relying only on reviews of others (as they might be fake). If I cannot personally visit the accommodations, I need to ask a pastor or youth pastor or trusted friend who lives in the area to actually go to the venue to check it out.

Next, I suggest being borderline fanatical about safety and proper supervision in travel situations. *Especially if you have just recently had any issues.* If I had another "problem" on the next retreat, my job would have likely been in jeopardy.

Perhaps the best thing I learned was that you should always make sure that someone on the youth staff, in a traveling situation, has great credibility in the eyes of the congregation. Then it would not just be *your* word if there is explaining to do. I can't imagine what would have happened without Sam.

STORY 39: LES, THE ANARCHIST
by Les Christie

During a youth group all-nighter, I organized a Polaroid (pre-digital era) camera scavenger hunt.

Each carload of adults and teens got a Polaroid camera and a list of pictures to take. The lists required situations like being in a police car and being stuffed into a laundromat clothes dryer. You know... *fun* stuff.

I had our guest speaker and four high schoolers in my car. It was one in the morning, and we'd just finished taking a picture of our group crammed into one of the old-fashioned, enclosed telephone booths.

We were in the parking lot of a local department store to get a picture of the teens on a horsey ride when two police cars pulled up with lights flashing.

They asked who was in charge. When I stepped forward, they leaned me against a police car and frisked me. The teens and our guest speaker were lined up against a wall.

Three more police cars arrived from neighboring districts. Now I started to get worried, and I tried explaining to an officer who we were and what we were doing. The officer then informed me that a neighbor near the telephone booth had seen a flash of light and phoned in to report that some teens had blown up the booth.

I knew it had simply been the camera flash, but the week before, someone had blown up a telephone booth in that area. The police were taking no chances.

They let us go, and the group I was with doesn't remember a single other thing from that event.

STORY 40: BOOKING BUSES (TO FORGET IS HUMAN)
by Stephanie Boyce

I just forgot.

I had just been promoted from copy girl to retreat girl. And I was super excited. I made the forms. I tracked the checks as they came in. I even made an alphabetical roster to check off each young person upon arrival. I sent a letter that told the teens what to pack, when to arrive, and what to expect. I really thought I had it all together.

I pride myself on my organizational skills. It was what I was known for as the administrative assistant for the youth pastor and this was my big break in taking on more responsibility.

Winter retreat is our biggest retreat of the year. We take about 70 teens and leaders to Wisconsin for a snow-filled weekend. Which means a lot of gear. Teens need snow pants, boots, hats, gloves, bedding, and, of course, a number of cute outfit changes for the ladies. All that equals a lot of people, and a lot of luggage. Which is why we rent a bus. Two, actually.

At 5:30 p.m., the youth started to arrive. I checked them off my color-coded roster and had the ladies label their bags with pink luggage tags. Check. The boys got blue tags. Double check. My faithful leaders showed up for the weekend. Triple check.

And the buses.

Where are the buses?

Has anyone seen the buses?

No check. No buses.

Seventy people, 140 bags, and no buses. Cue armpit sweat. I frantically looked for the bus company number. No answer. Fifteen minutes. Called again. No answer. Cue hot tears streaming down my face. Now we were late, and I was panicking. Five frantic redials and finally, a confirmation. Just not quite the one I was expecting. No buses were ordered.

I never confirmed the buses!

Epic fail. My first retreat planning and I forget one of the biggest details. Talk about humbling.

And now I had to tell Josh, the youth pastor, that there were no buses coming. In that moment, he had a choice. Josh could have scolded me, called me out, or been upset. He could have called off the retreat and sent everyone home. But he didn't. As I sat in the corner sniffling, he calmly took over. And after a few head counts, some division of cars, a few called-in favors from parents and leaders who weren't even planning on going to the retreat, he had it all figured out.

Mistakes sure have a way of knocking us off the pedestals we put ourselves on, don't they?

In the grand scheme of things, it wasn't a big deal. No one was hurt, no money was lost, or janitor upset. But it sure taught me a lot about people-first leadership, teamwork, humility, and planning.

Josh showed me what grace looked like. The way he treated me and reacted under pressure has shaped how I try to react to others. Because we all know mistakes are bound to happen in ministry. And, he didn't shame me in front of the team. He simply told everyone the buses didn't show. No one's fault. He was gentle with my heart and told me it would be okay.

We don't need to remind people of their failures. They already know, and usually that's enough. Josh did not stop giving me more responsibility either. In fact, years later when he transitioned to the role of senior pastor, he trusted me to run the entire ministry until we found a replacement.

It ended up taking a caravan of 16 drivers to get us up to Wisconsin for that trip. Not one of them made fun of me for the mistake. They just jumped in and made it happen. That's what team looks like.

DON'T DO THIS

"We had a pool party at the end of the summer and a bunch of the youth brought friends (as is the norm). And people, of course, were in bathing suits (as is the norm). A few months later I saw a girl in church who had been a guest at the party. I don't even know what all I was trying to say, but my brain short-circuited and mixed it all up. I ended up blurting out, 'Hey! Good to see you! I didn't recognize you with clothes on!' "

Jonathan Hobbs

And because of the cool conversations the leaders ended up having in their cars with such small groups of teens, we decided for the next few years that driving them—as opposed to taking the buses—was better. Leaders bonded with the youth, and we saved some money. We turned plan B into plan A.

We now take buses because it is safer and logistically easier. And, I always remember to confirm they are coming. But every year I sweat just a bit until they pull up.

STORY 41: IN THE SPIRIT OF PUBLIC SERVICE
by Les Christie

One of my first youth groups did service projects for the city of Garden Grove, California. We picked up trash and distributed food to needy families—both without any mishap. The city was pleased, and we were proud. We were ready for more.

Between the church building and the local high school was the Garden Grove Freeway. Beneath the freeway was a pedestrian tunnel. The tunnel, which was a youth thoroughfare, was full of graffiti and drawings.

I proposed that our youth group repaint the tunnel, and the mayor was delighted to accept. The city had to paint the tunnel twice a year, and they had us test a new game plan. We were given 130 large cans of spray paint and told to spray vertical lines up and down the length of the tunnel. That way, even if someone wrote graffiti on the walls later, the stripes would make the graffiti difficult to see.

Twenty-three youth showed up at the tunnel Sunday afternoon. I got them started and then left them with four adult volunteer sponsors.

The phone rang early on Monday morning. The mayor wanted me to meet him at the tunnel that morning. From the tone of his voice, I suspected he wasn't planning to present me with a service award.

As I arrived I saw the problem. The youth had painted the stripes as asked. Then they'd graced the walls with their *own* graffiti. Everywhere I looked, I saw such sentiments as, "Jesus is the answer," and "God loves you." One teen had written the entire chapter of Acts 3 on the floor of the tunnel.

The city officials somehow failed to appreciate the creativity.

STORY 42: CONCERT CATASTROPHE
by Len Kageler

Even though this happened ten years ago, it is still painful just to
think about. My heart and vision were right, but (yikes) it didn't work
out anything like I thought it would.

I interviewed with and accepted the call of a church to be their youth
pastor in November, with a projected start date of mid-February. My
mind began working overtime on ways to have a strong first year. I
had the mission/vision/core values and strategy thing down pretty
well, and that actually led me to start planning a major outreach event
there for my first October. I figured by then we'd have a core of teens
who were ready to invite friends to something really cool and work
hard to pull the whole thing off.

So, in December, I made the arrangements for a very well-known
Christian female (rock star) singer to come with her band and dance
team for an October outreach concert. I was pleased to get that
accomplished in such a short time, because I knew that people like
her generally were booked two to three years in advance. Contract
signed, I knew I could work on the rest of the details once I actually
arrived on the scene at my new church.

In the next ten months many things went wrong. The slick promo
posters they promised didn't arrive until one week before the concert.
I was shocked by the specificity and complexity of their light and

sound requirements, and I worked to find a local provider at a reasonable cost. The band manager, two weeks before the concert, fired my provider and hired a different one. I learned from my own youth group and from the youth pastors in the area that "Christian contemporary music" was kind of a foreign idea in the area.

The day of the concert was horrible. The sound and light people arrived to set up at four in the afternoon instead of nine o'clock that morning, and we quickly found out the middle school auditorium didn't have enough electrical power for their systems. So, at 4:30 p.m., I was tracking down the school district head electrician. The good news was he agreed to run cable from the main something-or-other to the auditorium, but the bad news was he that he charged $100 per hour.

The singer and nine-member band flew in from Nashville and were taken to their hotel. Meanwhile, two of my youth group teens accompanied the vans that went to pick them and their stuff up. These two came to the auditorium while we were (frantically now) setting up and reported, "She's a witch. What a stuck-up snob!"

DON'T DO THIS

"I interned at a church all through college. I realized that the education level there was maybe a little higher than most places when I was giving a Sunday school lesson and one of the fifth graders corrected my Latin."

Daniel Garrison Edwards

The evening of the concert was worse yet. The band arrived on time but the sound and light people weren't ready. When I did a mental survey of the entourage, I asked their road manager, "Where are the dancers your promo stuff bragged about?"

"Oh, that was last year's show. We don't have them anymore."

The sound check started at eight o'clock, when the concert was supposed to begin. So, we had 450-500 people standing outside for over an hour. (Said a huge thank-you to God that it wasn't raining and that he gave me the foresight to hire local police for security. Police presence did have a calming effect on the impatient youth.)

The concert finally started at nine that night. Financially our break-even point was 750 people. I had hoped and prayed for 1,000. We had 500, max. I realized we would lose at least $6,000 that night.

There went my youth budget for the year, if not my life.

But I consoled myself in that it would all be worth it for the kingdom harvest we were about to experience.

The audience was enjoying the concert, but at about the 45-minute mark, Ms. Star Singer began giving her "talk" and then her "invitation." I assumed this was the halfway point in the program. The only teens who "came forward" were my youth leadership team teens, who we had agreed would come up to counsel the others who came forward. Not one person made any response to the gospel presentation. The final song was sung and it was over and done at ten.

It was just one hour long.

Apparently I had no business being a concert promoter.

STORY 43: THE BLIND DATE

by Jonathan Hobbs

I moved to New Mexico for my first full-time job in youth ministry in a small isolated town. I didn't know a single soul, so was pleased to meet Jesse, a guy from my church. Jesse was loud, overly optimistic, occasionally inappropriate, and used Southern sayings that made no sense (e.g., "I'm happier than a chicken on St. Patty's Day!").

I liked him immediately.

I was visiting Jesse's office one day, and he asked if I'd "met someone" yet. I think the congregation figured that if I was going to stay long term, they'd probably have to "get me hitched" sooner than later. So this was a question I was asked pretty often.

When I told Jesse I hadn't dated anyone since my arrival, I found he had already done some homework. He took me out of his office, and we walked to hair salon next door.

"*Pamela!*" Jesse shouted. "This is the fella I told ya's about!" We walked over and I shook her hand. "Pam here cuts my hair. I happened to mention you just moving to town a few months ago and how you're awesome, and boy I'd love to find you a hot date. So then Pamela here has a brilliant idea…" he trailed off, kind of adding an *R* to the last word.

Pam picked up from there: "So I said, 'Well, what about my daughter

Rose?' " As Pam finished speaking, she pointed to a picture on her counter.

W*hoa…* Hello, Rose! (She was gorgeous… or at least the picture of her was.) I was suddenly *very* interested and became incredibly fascinated with Pam, Rose, Rose's dad, the family dog, and anything else Pam wanted to talk about. Turned out Rose was a junior taking classes at the junior college in town. Pam said I was a little older than Rose, but that Rose was mature and tended to date older guys. Knowing I was a youth pastor, Pam said she'd be delighted if I called and asked her daughter to dinner.

Boom! Win!

I called Rose. We chatted. I made stupid jokes. She laughed. We decided to get together and have dinner at my house that Friday night. I'd cook. She'd bring the movie.

After eating, we sat down to watch the movie, which is actually on the list of first-date don'ts. (Two people watching a movie at home doesn't help either of them get to know each other.) The movie also turned out to be so-so, and I was feeling awkward about how little conversation we'd had. So I was committed to more conversation.

At some point, the topic of school came up. I told her that I heard she was taking classes over at the junior college, and I asked her to clarify something that confused me. Her mom had said she was a "junior," but later I realized that there was no such thing as a junior at a two-year college.

"Oh, yeah," she replied, "I take a couple classes there. I'm hoping to attend there once I graduate."

Suddenly I could hear my heart beat… *Dear Lord, please let her not mean what I think she mea*—"Graduate?"

"Yeah… I'll graduate high school next year. I'm a junior now and I want to go to the junior college. They have a program for people that want to be hairdressers. I want to work at my mom's salon someday."

Oh no… no, no… nooooo. (*Heart beat… Heart beat…*) She was a high school student.

I have no memory of how I ended the evening. I might have faked a coughing spasm or a mild stroke. Or I might have actually *had* a mild stroke. I just know I went from "hoping for a kiss" to "hoping to keep my job."

I talked with Jesse the next day: "Dude… she is a *high school student!*"

He looked confused. "So you feel like you wouldn't have enough in common?"

I'm not sure exactly what lesson I learned from this little adventure, but if you're a youth director in your early twenties and you're getting set up on a date… *clarify* the person's age (and any other details you deem necessary to know). I think it's important to know that when you move to a completely different area of the country there are many things that might be different. The cultural learning curve is steep, and it's not a bad idea to take a couple of months to just try and get the lay of the land.

And if all of that doesn't apply to you, well… I just hope the story made you laugh.

Epilogue: *I only lasted 11 months at that church. Classic case of young youth director making a bunch of errors paired with a church with very little patience for it. They did their best, but I just wasn't a good fit.*

STORY 44: "DON'T CARS FLOAT?"
by Les Christie

A few months after I went on staff at Eastside Christian Church, an adult volunteer named Al suggested they take the youth group water-skiing. I'd never been water-skiing, but Al had a station wagon and boat, so I said, "Sure."

When we got to the lake, Al asked me to back the station wagon up so he could get the boat in the water. I'd never done that before either, but I agreed. That's when problems developed.

While the station wagon was backing up, the boat trailer began to jackknife. Al signaled for me to turn one way and then the other, but still the boat wasn't where it needed to be. If only we could get the trailer a few inches further into the lake, the boat would float. At this point the station wagon's back wheels were in the water, but Al kept signaling me to back up. So I kept backing up.

I ended up backing the car so far into the water that it began to float. It didn't float for long, though. As water cascaded into the station wagon, I had to swim out the window to safety.

Al eventually had to sell the car because it smelled so bad. After less than three months at a church, I had destroyed an adult volunteer's car. That has to be some sort of a record.

The good news: For eight years, Al continued to be a volunteer. He didn't get mad, and he hung in there with me. The bad news: Al was *always* telling that story. And it didn't do much to build my credibility with the youth group.

Be careful about taking on tasks you don't know how to complete. It may be a clear sign that it's someone else's ministry to do—or that you shouldn't go there at all.

STORY 45: BAD MOVIE EDITING
by Darrell Pearson

It was common practice for us to build our junior high camp themes around a film (16mm rentals, before video!). On Wednesday evening of camp, we would have movie night and show whatever film we based the programming on. On this particular year, my senior high director, Jim Hancock (now a writer and filmmaker), suggested *Breaking Away*. This is a movie that time has somewhat forgotten, but it was quite popular back in the day. It's sort of a coming-of-age story and centers a lot around the sport of biking.

We used the bike-racing theme for the camp. The planning came together nicely, and we were excited about the next few days. But early in the camp week Jim started rethinking his suggestion, as he was slowly recalling questionable scenes and dialog. This may sound odd to modern ears, but you have to remember—watching a movie wasn't as simple back then. It took special equipment! So he and I sat down, watched it, and decided we couldn't show it. There were just too many times where inappropriate language was used, and there were a couple scenes that I didn't feel comfortable showing to junior high students.

When we announced this decision at our morning staff meeting, the counselors hit the wall. Movie night was the big "easy" night of the week. Their protests were passionate enough to make rethink my decision. I chose to watch it again, and I made notes for each questionable scene in the film. On movie night, I sat at the film projector with my notepad and got ready to physically edit each inappropriate section live.

Needless to say, I blew it. I missed a number of rough swear words, turning off the sound a split second too late, making the movie go completely quiet after the swear word, giving it added emphasis.

I got nervous as youth and counselors were increasingly loving my misses. I knew that the roughest scene in the movie was one where two high school boys in a car pass the local college and watch a well-endowed girl jogging. Since their entire conversation was questionable, I decided to simply turn off the audio for the entire scene. This meant we all sat in complete silence and watched her run and bounce, then tried to imagine what the boys were talking about, then it was back to watching her run, bounce, then back in the car again.

It had made everything worse.

The youth were screaming for the audio, and counselors were falling apart laughing hysterically.

When I thought the scene was over, I turned up the volume again, just in time for the word *tits* to be heard all by itself… In a moment of complete panic, I turned the audio off again… adding an even higher level of emphasis to the word.

It became the word of the week of course. I worried about getting the dreaded calls from parents following the camp, but none ever came.

DON'T DO THIS

"I dictated an email to one of our associate pastors saying, 'I'll be in my office sitting by myself, stop by anytime.' He responded saying he could bring me toilet paper and a change of pants if I needed…

Not getting the joke, I checked the email that I sent and apparently 'sitting by' was changed into something else….

Thanks, smartphone… Well played."

Jonathan Hobbs

STORY 46: GETTING TO SECOND BASE WITH STRANGERS ON THE BEACH
by MaryAnn Alderfer

Editor's Note: *This story is from the youth's perspective, but we thought it was hilarious and had to be shared. We also wanted to make sure this never happens again. Read, enjoy, and learn.*

When I was in high school I attended a week-long evangelism camp that was held near a popular beach. Part of our day was spent learning about apologetics and how to answer tricky questions such as "Why would a good God allow bad things to happen to people?" Part of the day was spent crafting our personal testimonies and practicing them so we felt ready to share them with others. After some prayer and encouragement from our leaders, we were sent out in groups to the boardwalk where we talked to people about Jesus.

Whatever your opinion about street evangelism and open-air ministry in general, I look back on that camp as a valuable part of my faith formation. I'm not even sure if I'm completely comfortable with that kind of evangelism model, but I know I grew in my faith over those seven days. It helped me clarify my own "story" up to that point, and I hope it planted seeds in the hearts of the people we spoke with.

However, the camp leadership made one small mistake in their planning. They forgot to double-check youth culture when they crafted a little metric they asked us to use to demonstrate how our conversations had gone with the people we met.

190

I'll never forget when they got us all in the room and explained the "system" we would use for the week. "We want you to be able to easily communicate to one another about how far you got with people you met on the beach and boardwalk."

A feeling of concern passed through me. I was a pretty sheltered kid, but the way the leader said "how far you got" was a little too close to the way I'd heard other teenagers talk about how far *physically* they had gone with their boyfriend or girlfriend (or a random hookup). It was slightly funnier since the speaker mentioned "people you meet on the beach" which just sounded even more like a teen love story movie plot. But then the speaker kept going… and it got worse.

Much worse.

"If the person you talked to on the beach answered the question regarding where they thought they would go after they died… we say you 'got to first base.' If the person let you share your testimony, well then you got to 'second base.' Congratulations!"

I sank lower in my seat and tried not to look at anyone around me… This had to be a joke…

I don't remember what third base was, but getting them to pray the Sinner's Prayer was a "homerun." The youth pastor ended his talk—using a very serious/encouraging tone—saying, "I want you all to go out there this week and hit a homerun with strangers on the boardwalk! Go *all the way, people!*" I think he was expecting us to end with a giant cheer… or a slow clap… or something. We all just sat in a mild state of shock. If nothing else, it distracted from the point they were trying to make.

Looking back, I honestly wonder if the youth pastors in charge did that on purpose. Like… maybe someone lost a bet? Because the other option is that they were clueless. And I'm not sure which is the bigger fail.

SECTION V: REFLECTIONS

Rocky @yorocko   March 30
Before I took over, youth work trips took 15 kids. My first took nine. My second is taking six (with two on the fence). #youthministryfail

Reading and thinking about the stories in this section makes us want to drop to our knees and thank God for his grace, mercy, and protection!

Thank God for Sam, the bus driver/elder who explained to the parents how the overnight in a house of prostitution came about. He had so much credibility nobody crusaded for Len's dismissal. Thank God for the patient and longsuffering youth pastor, Stephanie's boss, who didn't tell anyone of her failure to order the buses, and instead— with a cheerful heart—informed the group the buses "just didn't show" before arranging for private car and van transportation. And thank God Jonathan's inadvertent blind date with a high schooler was in a part of the country where it was not uncommon at the time for high school girls to date much older guys.

If nothing else, these stories remind us that even when our failures defy categorization there is a loving Heavenly Father in the background—who himself defies categorization—guiding, protecting, and gently (or not so gently) forming us. We have both been on the receiving end of so much human grace, mercy, forgiveness, and tempered love, it serves to not only help us to remember our mistakes and failures so as not to repeat them, but to extend that same grace, mercy, and reality-based love to those around us.

Reflection and Discussion Questions

1. Which of these stories do you find most shocking or amazing? Why?

2.   Which of these stories could you most see yourself in?

3.   Can you think of other mistake stories of your own—or of other people you know in ministry—that are as remarkable as these?

4.   Reflect on or discuss with others one mistake you have made that makes you grateful for God's (sometimes miraculous) mercy.

5.   If you have had the opportunity to extend grace/mercy/love to someone in ministry who has failed or made a mistake, share that story.

Major Project Ideas for the Classroom

1.   Identify which story in each of the five sections hit you the hardest or were most helpful to you. Write a paper in five sections, one section for each of the sections of this book. In each section of your paper, identify the major lesson learned. Identify some of the emotions that were present (stated or implied). Identify situations in your future where you yourself may be vulnerable to make a similar mistake.

2.   In the previous assignments you explored many websites and book resources. Go back and review each one. Which three of these will be the most helpful to you in future ministry, and why? Write a two-page review of your favorite resource.

AFTERWORD: ONE FINAL THOUGHT

by J. R. Briggs

> "But he said to me, 'My grace is sufficient for you,
> for my power is made perfect in weakness.' Therefore
> I will boast all the more gladly of my weaknesses, so
> that the power of Christ may rest upon me. For the
> sake of Christ, then, I am content with weaknesses,
> insults, hardships, persecutions, and calamities.
> For when I am weak, then I am strong."
>
> — 2 Corinthians 12: 9-10

I live in a suburb just north of Philadelphia, Pennsylvania, where soil is so rich that, as the saying goes, if you can't grow a garden here, it ain't the garden's fault. A few years ago on Mother's Day, my wife wanted to spend Sunday afternoon planting a small vegetable garden in our backyard. Our oldest son, who was three at the time, wanted to help. He pulled on his boots and gloves, grabbed his toy trowel, and helped mommy in the garden. After several minutes, I called him in, cleaned him up, and put him down for his afternoon nap. I returned to his room 90 minutes later when I heard him stirring, and he opened his eyes to ask with childish excitement, "Daddy, are the vegetables ready yet?"

I chuckled at his cute and innocent question. I explained to him that growing vegetables doesn't work that way; it takes a long time for us to see anything come of our work in the garden and we have to be patient. My son was devastated. In the midst of this interaction, I had the simple yet jolting realization: As a pastor, I ask this question of God all the time. *God, I've worked so hard. When will I be successful? Why aren't the ministry vegetables ready yet?* Who knows, maybe you ask that question too.

Ministry books and conferences often focus on the wrong things. After finishing the last page of a book or sitting on the flight back from a conference, it can be tempting to develop a list of action items and next steps for us to accomplish when we get home.

I'm all for growth and learning. Long ago I made a personal commitment to remain a hungry life-long learner. But oftentimes, these types of ministry books and conferences can breed unhealthy ambitions and lead to a subtle but damaging focus on what we *do* for God—and ultimately what that might mean for us when we do it well. If we're truly honest with ourselves, we might admit that oftentimes our deep motivation is to grow a garden full of large and impressive vegetables—and quickly too.

What's refreshing about a book like this one is that it doesn't leave you with a laundry list of to-do items for how to fix your church or how to lead a fail-proof youth ministry. Instead, it invites us to learn from others who have experienced what ministerial gardening is in its truest sense (and are still in the learning process).

Spiritual gardening is fraught with failure and requires excruciating patience. In many ways, this is deeply refreshing. I've interacted with many kingdom leaders who are spiritually dry and exhausted, feel the weight of deep insecurity, wrestle with deep shame, and are caught in what I call "the insufficiency of enoughness."

Leaders who feel like they are not smart enough.
Not speaking at enough conferences or events.
Not growing a big enough youth group.
Not driven enough.
Not retweeted enough.

There are far too many places within Christian ministry that encourage us to spread our peacock feathers and compare ourselves with other pastors and ministries—mostly via the measuring sticks of attendance, budget, and the size of our facilities or events. I hope that in reading these pages you've found freedom and permission to resist the temptation of tracking the scorecard of ministry comparison. I hope you've found these pages are filled with stories of transparency and weakness that don't keep us from faithful ministry, but actually lead us further into it.

The good news for broken and deeply imperfect kingdom leaders like you and me is this: *Because the tomb is empty, the pressure is off.* Let that sink in for a moment. At the end of your days, when you stand face to face with your Creator, he will not say to you, "Well done good and *successful* servant." Jesus will never say to you, "What did you do with what I did *not* give to you?" And Jesus certainly won't ask you, "Why weren't you like that *other* pastor down the street?"

You are not called to be successful for Jesus; you are called to be faithful. We have to come to believe that God is more interested in what he is doing in us and through us than how well we manage or grow our ministries. Failures and mistakes are a part of the reality of ministry—and life. They are an invitation to grace and an opportunity to deepen intimacy with the God of the Universe.

The pressure is off. The tomb is empty.

Many of us are scared of failure because we have an inaccurate understanding of ministry success. In the introduction of his wonderful book *Working the Angles*, Eugene Peterson writes, "The biblical fact is there are no successful churches. There are, instead, communities of sinners, gathered before God week after week in towns and villages all over the world. The Holy Spirit gathers them and does his work in them. In these communities of sinners, one of the sinners is called pastor and given a designated responsibility to keep the community attentive to God."[20]

There are no successful churches, no successful ministries, no successful youth ministry programs. Peterson's thoughts force us to reconsider—and redefine—our concept of ministry failure and success. The Apostle Paul experienced the tender yet direct message that God's grace is sufficient for him. And for *all* people. Good news: This also includes pastors. This is why we—especially as kingdom leaders—can be honest about our weaknesses, failures, mistakes, and calamities. Paul says we can actually brag about our failures and weaknesses. By doing so, the love of God comes rushing in.

---

20. Peterson, Eugene. *Working the Angles: The Shape of Pastoral Integrity* (Grand Rapids: Eerdmans, 1989).

No matter your failures.
No matter your mistakes.
No matter the severity or amount of your sin.
No matter how far you've fallen.
God's grace is sufficient—even for you.
Because the tomb is empty. The pressure is off.

J. R. Briggs
Pastor of The Renew Community
Founder of Kairos Partnerships
Author of *Fail: Finding Hope and Grace in the Midst of Ministry Failure*[21]

21. Brigs, J. R. *Fail: Finding Hope and Grace in the Midst of Ministry Failure* (Downers Grove, IL: InterVarsity, 2014).

CONTRIBUTOR BIOS

Along with co-editors Len Kageler and Jonathan Hobbs, the following people contributed to this book:

MaryAnn Alderfer

MaryAnn Alderfer grew up as the daughter of a youth pastor. She has a BA in Elementary Education and worked for a Christian School in Southeast Pennsylvania. She now serves on the Children's Ministry staff at her church. She and her husband Dave keep busy raising their two energetic boys, Aaron and Timothy.

Ron Belsterling

Ron Belsterling (PhD) is a Professor of Youth Ministry at Lancaster Bible College. Ron has a youth ministry background in church-based youth ministry as well as Young Life. He is a popular retreat, camp, and conference speaker.

Alison Blanchet

Alison Blanchet is currently a youth minister in Panama City, Florida, but grew up in Hilton Head, South Carolina. After graduating from Franciscan University in Steubenville, Ohio, she spent two years as a lay missionary with the Society of Our Lady of the Most Holy Trinity in Belize, Central America. She enjoys chocolate, coffee, and thrift stores. She does not like cats or food on a stick. She is a regular contributor to LifeTeen.com and author of *Gifted: Unleashing the Power of Confirmation.* Follow her on twitter at @alisongriz or at http://www.teamcatholic.blogspot.com.

Stefanie Boyce

Stefanie Boyce is a writer who shares her journey of going "from type A to plan B" on her blog, stephanieboyce.com. She is no stranger to the pain and beauty of this world, and the tension that comes from living in the midst of both. She has spent ten years loving and serving high school students at Immanuel Church in Gurnee, Illinois, most recently as Interim Director of Youth Ministry. She is currently sharing her creative passion and talents with Immanuel as Director of Guest Relations. She is married to Justin, and together they have three beautiful children.

Les Christie

Les Christie is a national speaker and youth ministry veteran. He chairs the Youth Ministry Department at William Jessup University in Rocklin, California, and is the author of several books, including *When Church Kids Go Bad, What If...?, Have You Ever...?, Unfinished Sentences, Gimme Five,* and *Best-Ever Games for Youth Ministry.*

Chap Clark

Chap Clark (PhD, University of Denver) is Professor of Youth, Family, and Culture and Coordinator of Fuller Studio at Fuller Theological Seminary. Chap is president of ParenTeen™ (parenteen.com), a frequent speaker, consultant, and author. He was formerly senior editor of *YouthWorker Journal*, a *Sojourner* contributing writer and "Red Letter Communicator," and is the author or co-author of over 23 books.

Megan DeHaven

Since 2008, Megan DeHaven has served as the Director of Children and Youth Ministries at Bethany Colligate Presbyterian Church, which is the church she grew up attending. She graduated from Gordon College in 2008, with a degree in political science. Along with her husband, Mike, and daughter, Nora, she finds joy in the beautiful chaos that is living life for Christ.

Mark DeVries

Mark DeVries founded Youth Ministry Architects in 2002, and since 1986, he has served as the Associate Pastor for Youth and Their Families at First Presbyterian Church in Nashville, Tennessee, where he continues to oversee the youth ministry on a part-time basis. Mark has trained youth workers across the world and has guest lectured at many colleges and seminaries, including Princeton Seminary and Vanderbilt Divinity School.

Amy Jacober

Amy Jacober serves locally and nationally in youth ministry and has done so for a long time. When not at youth group or teaching, she is raising three small children or playing board games. She is the author of *Adolescent Journey* and the forthcoming *Redefining Perfect: Theology and Disability*.

Alisa Laska

Alisa Laska is a writer and 15-year veteran of youth and preteen ministry. She has a Masters in Theological Studies from Palmer Theological Seminary and has shared Jesus with students in three churches on the East Coast. She has written articles for *Youthworker Journal* and has published her writing and photography on getsparked.org. She enjoys encouraging other youth workers and writers and spending time with her baby and four-year-old son.

Tic Long

Tic Long is the Executive Pastor of Journey Community Church of La Mesa, California, and continues to be a presenter at youth worker gatherings. He helped lead Youth Specialties for 30 years and is known for his caring heart for youth workers.

Brock Morgan

For six years Brock Morgan was a member of the Youth Specialties One-Day national speaking team and has been working with youth for over 23 years. He is a popular speaker for camps, retreats, and conferences and has written for various magazines, co-authored *Parent's Guide to Teenage Guys* with Mark Oestreicher, and is the author of *Youth Ministry in a Post-Christian World*. You can visit his website at brockmorgan.com.

Mark Oestreicher

Mark (Marko) Oestreicher is a veteran youth worker and founding partner in The Youth Cartel, providing resources, training, and coaching for church youth workers. The author of dozens of books, including *Youth Ministry 3.0*, and *Hopecasting: Finding, Keeping and Sharing the Things Unseen*, Marko is a sought after speaker, writer, and consultant. Marko lives in San Diego with his wife, Jeannie, and young adult and teenage children, Riley and Max. Visit Marko's blog at whyismarko.com.

Darrell Pearson
Darrell Pearson is Associate Professor and Department Chair of Youth Ministries at Eastern University. His life-long ministry interest has been working with middle school students. Along with equipping college students to do the same, he volunteers with the youth group at a Chinese congregation in the Philadelphia area.

Andrew Root
Andy Root is the Olson Baalson Associate Professor of Youth and Family Studies at Luther Seminary (St. Paul, Minnesota) church, and culture (all with a deep theological bent) at Luther Seminary in St. Paul, Minnesota. He has written ten books and two more are on the way. His speaking and teaching in the field of youth ministry has increasingly taken him to the UK and beyond.

Ryan Sidhom
Ryan Sidhom dedicated his life to the ministry in the year 2000, and has been chasing after Jesus ever since. He has worked as a youth and college pastor, a music minister, an associate pastor, and "tech guy." He has had the opportunity to speak at several different youth outreach events, and he loves connecting with and communicating with teens. His first love is God, and his second love is his beautiful wife. All of his other loves can be found in either the meat or cheese food groups.

Jeff Smyth
Jeff Smyth has been doing youth ministry for 17 years. He and his wife have been married for 14 years and have one son, Nathan. Jeff's recent journey has focused on family, caregiving, youth ministry, and leadership. You can follow Jeff on Twitter/Instagram at @jeffsmyth and read his blog at jeffsmyth.wordpress.com.

To the authors who chose to withhold their names. We know that the stories you shared were hard to tell, and we pray that your transparency will lead to continued healing for you and also be a blessing for all who read this book. Thank you!

Also, a big thank you to all the authors of the shorter stories used as sidebars throughout the book.

Jonathan Hobbs | Twitter: @jonhobbstweets

Jonathan Hobbs has worked in professional youth ministry for over 17 years, including churches in New Jersey, New Mexico, South Carolina, and Pennsylvania. He has spoken and/or led worship for multiple camps, retreats, and events around the country. He took karate in high school because he thought it would help make him cool. He was wrong. Jonathan and his wife, Carolyn, have two beautiful daughters, Kaylin and Julia. He loves golf, can skillfully juggle two balls, and does a halfway decent impression of Kermit the Frog.

Len Kageler | Twitter: @LenKageler

Len Kageler (PhD) is a Professor of Youth and Family Studies at Nyack College in Nyack, New York, and New York City. He is the author of nine other books, including *Youth Ministry in a Multifaith Society: Forming Christian Identity Among Skeptics, Syncretists, and Sincere Believers of Other Faiths* (InterVarsity, 2014). He is often a guest lecturer or seminar presenter at youth worker or academic gatherings in North America and the European Union. Len is a runner, a researcher and reader. He and his wife, Janet, enjoy hiking year round. And Len, when he backpacks with friends in winter, is famous for making good omelets while camping on snow.

Books, blog, and other things: www.LenKageler.squarespace.com.